HERE
BECAUSE WE'RE
QUEER

Inside the
Gay Liberation Front of
Washington, D.C.,
1970-72

Brian Miller

Washington, D.C.

Here Because We're Queer: Inside the Gay Liberation Front of Washington, D.C., 1970-72

First published in the United States of America in 2020 by Brian Miller

Second printing November 2020

Soft Cover: ISBN 978-0-578-72872-8

Ebook: ISBN 978-0-578-72871-1

Cover Design: Eric Seidman

Book Design: Judy Walker, judywalkerdesign.com

Printer: IngramSpark

Library of Congress Control Number:

2020914510

Cover and title page photo: Jim Lawrence, Paul Bartels, Bruce Pennington, Benton Quinn and Theodore Kirkland on parade in Manhattan in 1971 at the Christopher Street Liberation Day. (Photo: Rainbow History Project)
Back cover author photo: Franz Jantzen

HERE
BECAUSE WE'RE
QUEER

Stonewall Inn, Greenwich Village, New York, September 1969. (Photo: Diana Davies/The New York Public Library/CC BY=SA 3.0)

HERE
Because We're
QUEER

Gay Power to Gay People! The Stonewall riots in New York City exploded when patrons at a Greenwich Village gay bar fought back against police conducting a routine raid one June night in 1969. This incident started a movement that ultimately transformed American society—in laws, practices and attitudes. In New York, the first radical group to form in response to the riots was the Gay Liberation Front. Soon, GLF groups began to spring up across the country in cities large and small. Washington held its first GLF meeting on June 30, 1970.

GLF-DC's activities included protests, publications and communal living experiments. Although the group faded quickly, its attendees established an openly gay community and helped start some long-lasting institutions in Washington—Capital Pride, Whitman-Walker Health, the Metropolitan Community Church and Lambda Rising bookstore, to name a few.

Despite this legacy, the story of the D.C.'s Gay Liberation Front, hidden in the long shadow of gay pioneer Franklin Kameny and eclipsed by the well-organized Gay Activists Alliance (now GLAA), has gone largely unremarked. This work is an attempt to enlarge the historical record. More than a recounting of events, it's also a memoir.

I attended a handful of early GLF meetings and occasionally took part in political actions, where I confess I was little more than a warm body. And my interest in politics, never strong, fizzled long before GLF itself did. As a noncommittal, stubbornly independent, mildly depressed young man, I was simply not an activist. I wanted to live among the radicals, but I wasn't willing to commit to political action. I am not proud of my personality traits, nor of the immature, inexplicable behavior I sometimes engaged in. I was happy to remain quietly on the sidelines, listening as others held forth. And I was always ready to move on when faced with personal problems. I even left Washington twice during the period when GLF was active.

All in all, I am among the least qualified individuals to represent GLF. The story of GLF is not about me, so I have minimized my own story while recounting GLF's—though I still felt compelled to juxtapose my own aimless existence with the more idealistic activities of my fellows.

In 1994 I attended a reunion of GLF-DC and came face to face with the reality that veterans of the early '70s had begun to disappear, far too soon, mainly because of AIDS. I decided at that time to start recording survivors' memories to create a kind of GLF-DC archive. So began the long, intermittent oral history project that led to this publication. I assembled this microhistory from interviews with more than 50 participants, plus my own personal journal notes and memories, and contemporary news accounts. Wherever possible, I compared accounts to arrive at the most accurate record of what happened. This memoir/history, then, recalls my own thoughts, feelings and actions, and also draws on a range of other individual lives and how politics touched them.

Where incidents have been written about before—particularly Frank Kameny's 1971 run for nonvoting delegate to the U.S. House of Representatives and the "zap" of the American Psychiatric Association meeting that same year—I have kept my coverage somewhat perfunctory. All other material I treat more fully.

My research and writing of the GLF story revealed some recurring themes that deserve mention. Among them:

- Some gay bars blatantly discriminated against gay customers, while there was also a less acknowledged desire among some gays to socialize only with people like themselves.
- Long before the Internet age, early identity politics was rampant, with the now-familiar use of political correctness as a weapon in attacks on people having opinions different from one's own.

- Behind the public phalanx of angry gay radicals were individuals with sometimes surprising fears, ideals, spiritual needs, even confusions about sexual identity.
- The radical demands of African American activists and white gay activists reveal disturbingly wide social disparities that still exist.

I and many others remain proud to have been part of this brief period, and this memoir/history is an attempt to reveal why former radicals feel this way. I pay tribute to the activists of Gay Liberation Front of Washington, D.C.—with their own individual strengths and weaknesses—by presenting their voices and stories here.

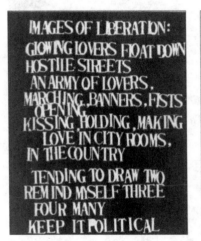 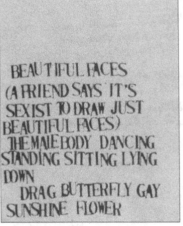

Motive (Gay Men's Issue and Last), *1972, "Images of Liberation"*
(Artwork: Fag Rag)

The Dupont Circle neighborhood provided a beautiful setting where people of all kinds could flourish. (Photo: emkaplin)

(Photo: Andrei Medvedev)

CHAPTER 1

Washington Waits for GLF

SITTING UP STRAIGHT as I could in front of a huge, old Underwood in June 1969, fingers poised on the keys and staring at a practice booklet of typing exercises, I didn't hear the distant thunder of Stonewall. A disturbance in a New York gay bar was not news in Baltimore. The only sounds I heard were the erratic tapping noises I was making.

At 24, and without fully understanding why, I needed change, and I set about making it happen—in short order I was preparing to move to a new city and a new job, and so a new life. I'd found work as an editorial assistant at an association in Washington, and I spent the summer before the move teaching myself how to type, which was a condition of getting the job. Within a year of my move, I fell in with the argumentative men and women of the Gay Liberation Front of Washington, D.C.

There had been signs early on in my development that my suburban Baltimore parents' expectations about producing a proper young man were not going as planned. As a child, I fell into giggling fits when my father tried to teach my brother and me how to hit a baseball, until finally he walked away in disgust. In first grade, I enjoyed going to a classmate's house after school, where we would play with her dolls; but mothers conferred, and the play dates ceased. Around age 14, I enjoyed styling my mother's hair, teasing it out of its outmoded 1950s bob and into a bouffant 1960s look. One evening she displayed my creation to her visiting girlfriend, who smiled too brightly and commented, "Maybe he'll turn out to be a *hairdresser*." In an instant, I understood the essence of her message, and my fun turned to shame.

When I eventually became aware that I was attracted to boys, I responded as any normal abnormal boy would do in the conformist 1950s: I suppressed and hid. I stumbled through the required dating rituals of the time, but with anxiety, lies, hurt feelings, ignorance and passivity. Increasingly, I felt trapped in an unhappy existence.

Silence cloaked the topic of homosexuality in the 1950s and early 1960s. It was simply not something one discussed in polite company. Of course, I heard and even repeated jokes about homosexuals. And I learned the ugly words to describe them—*queer, fairy, fruit, pansy, fag, cocksucker*—and dreaded being associated in any way with this category of humanity. But the hurtful names I learned on the street and in school could at least be attributed to immaturity and ignorance. Beyond the street was a steady drumbeat of acceptable name-calling, but here the words were *abnormal, decadent, immoral, unnatural.*

Such labeling was done by experts, and their loaded language was everywhere. Magazines and newspapers made it clear that I was at best a problem in search of a solution, at worst an evil menace to society. Or I was diseased, a pathological condition for which there was no real cure. I figured I was somewhere part of the mix of transvestite queens, compulsive sex psychopaths and "sadie-mashies," as a nominally empathetic *Washington Post* writer described the range of homosexuals in 1965.[1] I couldn't confide my confusion and anxiety to anyone. And how had this happened to me?

The various answers to this question came through loud and clear. *Time* magazine declared in 1953 that homosexuality is "a symptom of an underlying emotional disorder." Parents who notice signs of homosexuality in their son should take him to a psychiatrist who will show the boy how his "emotional growth has been stunted or twisted," and thus resolve the problem.[2]

But resolving the problem wasn't that simple. In 1956, a New York psychoanalyst posited that the adult homosexual "wallows in self-pity and continually provokes hostility to ensure himself more opportunities for self-pity…he is generally unreliable, in an essentially psychopathic way."[3] The same year, the *British Medical Journal* reported on research conducted on homosexual patients at a British mental hospital. Amazingly, what they found was that almost every male subject was no different physically from a normal man: "They were not unusually hippy, did not have overdeveloped breasts, their pubic hair grew in the normal male pattern."[4] (This research was the late flowering of a line of professional declarations that homosexuals were physically abnormal, for instance that lesbians had prominent clitorises and gay men had doglike penises.)[5] And in the late 1960s, psychiatrist Charles Socarides offered the theory that most homosexuals "show evidence of a 'screaming phenomenon'—screaming for an inordinately long time and beyond the age of 3 whenever their mother disappeared from behind the baby carriage or at night."[6]

Even months after Stonewall and the beginning of a more understanding era, *Time* magazine assured readers that despite the common misconception that homosexuals were all alike, there were in fact six categories of homosexual: blatant, secret lifer, desperate, adjusted, bisexual and situational-experimental. That tidy assortment seemed authoritative, but also confusing. Where did I fit in? The same issue of *Time* concluded, "While homosexuality is a *serious* and sometimes *crippling maladjustment*, research has made clear that it is no longer necessary or morally justifiable to treat all *inverts* as *outcasts*. The challenge to American society is simultaneously to devise civilized ways of *discouraging the condition* and to alleviate the *anguish* of those who cannot be helped, or do not wish to be" [italics mine].[7]

And let's not forget to add in the scorched-earth teachings of major religions.

Since the experts presented such a wide range of theories about homosexuality, I feel entitled to my own equally reasonable theories about a few of the many possible causes of my gayness—experiences that stirred changes inside me, enlarged my worldview, provided models, nudged me onward:

Hearing tenor William Tabbert's impassioned high notes in the song "Younger Than Springtime" on the *South Pacific* Broadway cast LP. Reading the novels of Mary Renault, with their re-creation of ancient Greek life and love. Steeping myself in the camp satire of Patrick Dennis's novel *Auntie Mame*. Seeing the dust-jacket portrait of Truman Capote on *Other Voices, Other Rooms*, looking like a 12-year-old being punished for misbehavior in Sunday school and gazing longingly into the reader's eyes for help.

Or maybe the movies did it, with their distinctive stars. Recessive, awkwardly sensitive young Anthony Perkins seemed a reflection of my misunderstood self. The subtle, sibilant presence of Vincent Price crept into my psyche; was I destined to be the suave, amused gentleman or the hideous monster lurking behind his crumbling façade? Was I the dazzling Blonde Venus that slowly emerges from inside a menacing gorilla suit in the form of serenely languid and androgynous Marlene Dietrich?

Certainly, the intended message of the movies, as they began to tackle the subject of homosexuality in the late 1950s, was more cautionary than tea and sympathy. The ads for one 1959 film cried, "*Suddenly, Last Summer,* Cathy knew she was being used for something evil!" Which meant, as audiences were to learn, that her doomed cousin was using her to attract boys for his own pleasure. (My perhaps prescient mother recommended the movie to me—and when I saw it, I didn't consciously understand it!) In *The Children's Hour* (1961), a suspected lesbian hangs herself. In *Advise and Consent* (1962), a former homosexual kills himself. In *The Fox* (1967), a lesbian is killed by a falling tree. In *The Sergeant* (1968), a closeted military man shoots himself. Incredibly, each new release, however dire its message, gave me more of the information I was hungry for and somehow felt to me like a brick in the foundation of a slowly emerging homosexual world. The price of progress—death—somehow seemed acceptable.

As a young man in college, and now clearly understanding myself to be homosexual, I knew of no way to find others. There was a hidden gay world, I was sure of it, but I knew of no way to reach it. Aside from the occasional acknowledging glance from a passing stranger—what did *that* mean?—all I knew was that a subculture existed, but you had to know the password, or break the code, or find a bar to go to.

Others, I later learned from Gay Liberation Front, had a wide range of experiences breaking into the gay world:

Stephen looked up "gay" in the phonebook and found the Gayety Buffet. It turned out to be just the ticket.

Peter in the suburbs decided not to go to college a virgin, so he went to Dupont Circle because he heard queers went there; he got picked up and had his first gay sex.

Kent's idea of gay life came out of a 1960s *Life* magazine article that included photographs of gay men on the street wearing big, fluffy sweaters; he bought a couple of huge sweaters to identify himself to others.

Bill discovered "correspondence clubs" through male nudist magazines. The subscription-based clubs were basically privately mailed personal ads. You wrote a letter, then met for sex. After a number of hookups, he started thinking about suicide.

I didn't even know where any gay bars were until, on a visit to Washington, a college friend happened to point out the Georgetown Grill. The Grill sat right on busy Wisconsin Avenue in the heart of Georgetown, not on some dark back street. The windows were discreetly shuttered at night. Staring at the bar that day, at age 21, I knew I would have to make the desperate passage into the gay world, and here.

One cold night, visiting D.C. from College Park, Maryland, I worked up the courage to go to the Grill. Terrified of being sexually assaulted yet needing to be in this milieu, I entered, then strode from the front door straight to the bar without looking right or left at the men sitting at tables or in banquettes. I ordered a beer and sat drinking for about 10 minutes, glancing nervously into the bar mirror to see if anyone was eyeing me. No one seemed to notice me. Then I did an about-face and marched to the front door. I made it out alive! I was not tempted to go to bars again for a few years.

But having crossed over, however clumsily, and having settled down a bit after college with a good job, I did start exploring Baltimore's gay bars, though with little success. Nothing seemed to work out. One brief relationship with a man who told me he was straight—but whose private behavior gave every indication otherwise—ended one evening after we'd dined at a downtown restaurant and were contentedly strolling the summer streets. I was talking about being gay, and he suddenly asked me not to talk so loudly. Passersby might hear. "But I'm queer!" I shouted in my own little pre-Stonewall explosion, amazed that he could think anyone on the anonymous city streets would care what we were. (It would be many years before my self-loathing "queer" would be reconditioned for more positive general usage.)

I began to realize just how discontented I'd become. I had passively followed an academic path to a career. But now a deep-seated resistance began to assert itself. Life was passing me by. I was a middle-class adult, but I'd already missed the Summer of Love. I'd already started to assemble the right home furnishings, with a black leather sofa and stark white Formica cube tables, but part of me wanted a mattress on the floor. Instead of coat and tie, I wanted long hair and jeans, just like the students who were occupying college presidents' offices. I had missed some vital period of growth, and I would have it. I was willing to work for less money if it meant I could be free, and somehow Washington seemed the answer to my problems. Soon I found my first job there and began learning to type. I arrived in D.C. on the very weekend that young people were sliding around in the mud of Woodstock, N.Y.

A YEAR AFTER THE RIOTS that followed the assassination of the Rev. Martin Luther King Jr., a still-tense and socially uneasy Washington was heaving itself toward world-class status as a city. It was building a Kennedy Center. And late in 1969, construction began on the Metro system that would open in 1976. Soon, tunneling and demolition of buildings that were in the way began turning sites around town into hardhat camps. The streets and sidewalks near future Metro stations became wooden planking systems that subjected drivers who were determined to get through to a bumpy ride and the unnerving clanking of lumber. With fewer customers, the downtown shopping district faltered and nighttime streets became even more desolate.

Dupont Circle was the place to be. Physically, the neighborhood was (and is) a mishmash of late-19th-century townhouse styles, with an irregular profile that provided perpetual eye appeal. Small front yards and shade trees were everywhere. A few 1920s apartment buildings stood on street corners, and here and there, great mansions survived from the late 1800s, when the area was fashionable.

After World War II, the wealthy moved on, and many elegant townhouses were turned into boarding houses for returning veterans.[8] When the 1968 riots that followed the assassination of Dr. King ravaged the nearby 14th Street corridor from U Street northward, many whites fled and Dupont housing became more available and affordable. Young people, especially hippies and activists, happily joined the artists and office workers already living there.

A proper tone was in part maintained. Older Connecticut Avenue shopkeepers still offered ladies' hats, stationery, linens and high-end groceries to a dwindling trade. (Largely hidden from view, Alice Roosevelt Longworth, a ruler of Washington political and social circles from a long-gone era, still lived in her Massachusetts Avenue townhouse just off the circle.) Dupont even had its own fine art district, with several galleries showing and selling work.

But a less refined element had come along in the years of decline, and they frequented the sandwich shops and bars. One favorite haunt was the Ben Bow Irish pub. "Brooding like some funky, nasty old hen next to the Janus theaters,"[9] as the *Post's* Henry Allen described it, the raucous, dark and somewhat sticky bar attracted artists, rednecks, revolutionaries, motorcyclists, bureaucrats, panhandlers and the occasional drag queen.

Dupont Circle did not exactly roll out the red carpet for the baby boomer influx. Relatively few youth-oriented businesses opened to serve them, and you had to run over to Georgetown to find the cool clothes you wanted. But the message now seemed to be "we are all brothers and sisters." The air was often scented with the aroma of marijuana or, once in a while, the sharp taste of tear gas deployed to scatter antiwar demonstrators. People could get by on very little, and one could somehow find a place to crash. On the street, young people shared cigarettes and joints with strangers as a matter of camaraderie. (And years before a virtual army of unfortunate homeless people—some released from mental institutions—would set up individual begging stations along Connecticut Avenue, only a few familiar "characters" wandered around.)

The parkland expanse of Dupont Circle itself, with its classical fountain, was the hub of foot traffic for workers, students, tourists, activists, dope dealers and drunks. Guitars, drums and chess games cropped up. Conversation between strangers of all races seemed to have the potential to change young lives. Or you could just sit on a bench and watch.

The little corner drugstore at 1700 Connecticut Avenue, Schwartz's (which later became a Starbucks), was the neighborhood gathering spot, with a lunch counter manned by super-efficient Eddie and Charlie. Late Sunday morning breakfasts were a tradition there. Sunlight streamed in, creating a curtain of cigarette smoke as patrons pored over thick editions of the *Washington Post* and the *New York Times,* and people lingered at the few tables over hotcakes, bacon, eggs and coffee.

In this mixture of the staid and the drugged, everyone seemed to get along. And despite the baleful presence of Richard Nixon in the White House, and antiwar sentiment permeating the population, the city tried to make urban life work. Free rock concerts took place at P Street Beach (a corner of Rock Creek Park at 23rd and P streets NW), Farragut Square and the Sylvan Theater. And one summer evening I was surprised to happen upon the entire National Symphony Orchestra giving a concert by the Dupont Circle fountain—an enchanting idea even if the music was somewhat defeated by traffic noise.

I had decided on the seen-better-days Chateau Thierry apartment building at 20th and S streets the moment I noticed hippies sprawling out of a second-floor window over the building's entrance canopy. This is where I wanted to be, my Bohemia. So what if in summer I sweltered in my eighth-floor one-bedroom and if in winter the radiators clanked at night? So what if I had to take the stairs after the old elevator man went off duty for the night? So what if the kitchen appliances were antique? I could walk down stately Massachusetts Avenue to work. I had glorious sunlight waking me in the morning and—if I stuck my head out the bathroom window—a view of the Washington Monument.

Dining out was affordable. The Crystal City Restaurant, catty-corner across Connecticut Avenue from Schwartz's, provided a complete meal for $2. The homey Trio Restaurant on 17th Street had tiny booths and big waitresses who addressed regulars as "Hon," all overseen by wait-ress-cashier Margo MacGregor, who became a friend to many young gays. And for the seriously thrifty, Sholl's Cafeteria could not be beat if you could tolerate the cards placed on tables asserting, "Patriotism and religion make this a great place to work." The food served at these staple neighborhood restaurants was decent, plain American fare, and coffee came in two flavors: regular and decaf. Chinese food meant the Nanking on P Street. Greek meant the Astor on M.

Life was good, for a while. I had a 9-to-5 job that left me other-wise free; I was meeting young people at work; and I had access to all the movies, books and records I could possibly need. The nearby Janus

Theater had a restrained mosaic exterior on Connecticut Avenue and was forever showing the supposedly titillating Swedish movie *I Am Curious (Yellow)* when I moved to town. I was never curious enough to see it, but finally the theater began showing other art films. A bit further afield was the cheap repertory house the Circle Theater on Pennsylvania Avenue with its endless double features of old movies. And Discount Books, below the circle on Connecticut, had a huge selection of books and records. I would relax and grow into my intended self in this neighborhood.

About three weeks after I arrived in D.C., I decided that having a roommate would make life even more affordable. I went to a coworker's party for an arranged meeting with a young man who needed a place to stay. All was cool. Everyone smoked the hostess's lousy grass and sat on the floor staring at black-lighted Day-Glo posters as Isaac Hayes's hypnotic version of "Walk On By" encouraged the trippy mood from the record player. The next day I made the housing offer, and on the day the guy moved in, we smoked a joint, made love on the pallet he'd set up on the living room floor, and that was that. We became a couple.

So, I was making it all happen: Move to a new city, check. Get a new job, check. Get a lover, check (although I moved a little too fast on that last item, as I unhappily learned after a few weeks).

BEYOND MY OWN WORLD, a lot had happened to gay life in D.C. The witch-hunts of the Sen. Joseph McCarthy era, which ferreted out homosexuals as well as communists, were ancient history by now, but their legacy lingered. A 1953 presidential executive order had declared that homosexuality was a bar to a security clearance for federal government workers, and not simply because homosexuals could be targets for blackmailers. It also seemed, as one official told the *Washington Post*, that "they are emotionally immature and unstable, talk too much, and are highly susceptible to flattery."[10] The ban stayed in place until 1995, when President Bill Clinton signed an order that gave gays and lesbians access to classified government documents.[11] Meanwhile, government investigators felt free to ask suspected homosexual employees if they had ever engaged in acts of oral or anal copulation with others, and, if so, with whom.[12]

Occasionally a homosexual pushed back, and one of these was Franklin Kameny. In late 1957 Kameny, a Harvard-educated astronomer, had been fired from his job as a civilian employee at the Army Map Service because the government had information about his arrest in a San Francisco bus station men's room in 1956.[13] After unsuccessfully appealing his firing, an angry Kameny turned to activism. He helped found what came to be called the Mattachine Society of Washington (MSW) in 1961.[14]

Along with other homophile organizations such as Daughters of Bilitis, Mattachine worked quietly and systematically for civil rights for homosexuals. It published information about the rights of gays under D.C. law, including the useful facts that dancing together and showing affection were as legal among same-sex couples as they were between men and women. Transvestism was also legal. All well and good, except that on the street, many homosexuals found that "disorderly conduct" was a loosely defined category, which both policemen and judges might interpret broadly and harshly.[15]

Mattachine actions such as marching in front of the White House in the spring of 1965 were carefully staged for public consumption. As activist Lilli Vincenz said in an interview, everyone except Kameny had to use a pseudonym, and coat and tie were required for men, skirts or dresses for women. One important message of such carefully choreographed protests was respectability, and in fact, in a 1965 *Washington Post* interview, Kameny seemed eager to distance himself from "the 'flaming faggots' who swish along the street and the compulsive and potentially violent perverts who haunt public restrooms and parks."[16]

Kameny ran MSW, and he ruffled feathers. Authoritarian and intense by nature, he once got into a violent argument with Shirley Willer of Daughters of Bilitis New York, according to Vincenz. The two almost came to blows. "Frank's voice rose to a high C—he was so furious," she said. "And he started moving toward her as if to punch her," but others intervened just in time. He later had to write a letter of apology. "Very hard for him to swallow," said Vincenz.[17]

Kameny also had the impressive ability to speak with great clarity and force. His mental facility (and, I'm sure, planning and practice) allowed him to work his way through long, complex spoken sentences and reach the end grammatically intact. This skill added to his aura of au-

Ubiquitous Frank Kameny with gay marchers at an early-'70s antiwar demonstration. (Photo: Dirk Bakker)

thority and his ability to dominate a situation. And if his most characteristic public emotion was righteous anger, he also had an actor's instincts about maximum impact in a political moment, as well as a spark of wry humor.

Under Kameny's leadership, some discontent arose by the late 1960s in the small, secretive group. "Mattachine seemed to be for the elite," said Vincenz, "those people who were willing to use the channel of very respectable requests for change," in contrast to the civil disobedience used in the black civil rights movement. She also recalled that "Mattachine did not reach out to the average gay person who also wanted a social connection." (Kameny indeed had little interest in widening MSW's scope to include activities such as get-togethers, since he believed these diluted the main purpose of the group.)[18]

But Kameny was the go-to guy for anyone needing information or help with any kind of homosexual-related problem. He offered advice for people harassed by blackmailers, counseled on the military draft and security checks, advised on job dismissals based on homosexuality, and gave educational lectures—and much of his work was done gratis and behind the scenes.

MEANWHILE, CHANGE that had nothing to do with Mattachine was coming to the D.C. social scene: the advent of the superbar. In the late 1960s, men could choose among neighborhood bars such as the Georgetown Grill; the Chicken Hut, a piano bar on H Street NW; the multicultural "1832" in Adams-Morgan; and Johnnie's on Eighth Street SE. They could also visit the Hideaway, a basement bar with a jukebox at Ninth Street and Pennsylvania Avenue NW, across from FBI headquarters; the Brass Rail, featuring black drag performers; and Dolly's and the Naples Café, for drag and hustlers near the bus station. (There would not be gay bars in Dupont Circle for several more years.)

Women had limited choices. Perhaps the nicest bar was Jo-Anna's on Eighth Street SE. At the Rendezvous, on 10th Street NW, the femmes wore dresses, and the butches wore men's suits and ties, according to one patron. "If two butches got into an argument, you cleared out because one of them was going to come up with a knife or a gun," she added.[19] At the Amber Room (aka Steve's) at 14th Street and Park Road NW, dancing took place in a back room, and the bar had a buzzer system to alert patrons to break apart if authorities arrived.[20]

Bar patrons had to sit in order to drink, and bar employees routinely reprimanded any innocent who tried to walk with a drink in hand. Under D.C.'s liquor law, which was passed after Prohibition to limit drinking, "there were technically no bars in Washington, only restaurants that had liquor licenses," wrote journalist Lou Chibbaro Jr. "To ensure that the sale of liquor was secondary to food purchases, the law required patrons to be seated at a counter or table to drink beer and wine and only at a table to consume mixed drinks."[21] Establishments that were essentially bars offered limited and unappetizing menus, but still were required to have working kitchens.[22]

And as late as 1969, self-imposed prohibitions about same-sex dancing were sometimes still in place, despite the fact that the activity was legal. Cautious bar owners worried especially about customers touching while dancing and, as Chibbaro wrote, were "fearful that the vice squad would charge them with promoting lewd and immoral behavior,"[23] and thus endanger their liquor license.

But superbars essentially shoved all this regulation aside. The first to open, in 1969, was the Plus One, on Eighth Street SE. It was sleek, with an aluminum façade;[24] trendy, with empty gilded picture frames hung on the walls;[25] cheeky, with blackboards and chalk provided over urinals.[26] Activist Paul Kuntzler witnessed a telling incident there in May 1969, weeks before the Stonewall rebellion. A large group of gay men were lined up outside waiting to get in. That night a number of police cars converged on the bar from both ends of the block, and officers got out and walked toward the bar. People had routinely fled bars at the first hint of the cops arriving, according to Kuntzler, but "the people in line that night seemed almost oblivious to the police. They just continued their own conversations...The police went back to their cars and tried it all over again." Again, no reaction.[27] Perhaps the patrons had sensed the power provided by the money they spent and were done with intimidation tactics.

Within a few years, other superbars emerged: In May 1970, the Pier Nine (a converted warehouse at Buzzard Point off South Capitol Street) opened,[28] featuring Kit Kat Klub-style telephones on tables so patrons could call other tables. The nearby Lost and Found opened in October 1971.[29] The big bars had large dance floors and DJs operating great sound systems that enveloped patrons in pounding dance music. Hundreds of people lined up in their trendiest duds to experience the chic atmosphere. Doormen managed the crowds and checked IDs. The result was that with so many well-heeled patrons flocking to the bars—not insignificantly including more and more straight people eager to make the scene—the old proscriptions against dancing and walking with a drink became unenforceable.

Gay life was blossoming in Washington, yet despite the changes, it was not exactly liberated, even in 1970. The police had largely backed off, though entrapment was still a danger in Lafayette Square across from the White House, which had been a cruising area for many decades. But in general you knew the time-honored drill: Keep your head down. Blend in. Don't do anything foolhardy, like announcing your gayness to coworkers. Go subtler. Communicate with others you hoped were gay by, say, casually mentioning an old Bette Davis movie in conversation. Never camp it up. Camp was a sort of homo Esperanto, a universal insider way to establish connections; but too strong a vocal intonation or too many allusions to old movie queens might go too far. Instead, leave a pack of matches from a gay bar, unremarked, on your coffee table and see if there's any reaction. Careful—go beyond restrained signals and you could be in trouble.

BY MID-1970, I AGAIN WANTED change. My editorial job seemed humdrum, my love life was in the doldrums, and I got mugged at gunpoint on S Street.

Social problems and danger were never far away. By 1970, hippie culture around Dupont Circle had soured somewhat because of the increased presence of heroin and speed; more and more young runaways were around, and many of them, lacking money, turned to panhandling.[30] Perhaps emblematic of how far things had sunk was the once-grand Cairo Hotel, at 1615 Q Street. Opened in 1894, the ornate structure was now dilapidated inside and had become home to prostitutes, drug addicts, alcoholics[31] and the mentally disturbed.[32] I crossed the street when walking past it.

The world itself felt more ominous: In March a Weatherman bomb accidentally killed three people in New York, and in May the Kent State University shootings convinced me that "they" wanted to kill "us." Washington itself was less appealing. The summer was oppressive, and the air was sometimes thick with the inescapable stench of stewing animal parts wafted eastward from the Georgetown rendering plant. Anxious, I again felt a need to escape and make a new start elsewhere. When a woman from work said she and her husband needed help moving their household furnishings to San Diego, I decided to drive a truck across the country for them—and also to move to San Francisco. The glory days of Haight-Ashbury were long over, but San Francisco still exerted its pull.

I had no work lined up and no place to live, but there were crash pads to shelter newcomers, I could live off unemployment for a while, and things would somehow work out.

A few weeks before I left town, a friend persuaded me to go with him to Georgetown's Grace Episcopal Church for a meeting of the new Gay Liberation Front. He didn't want to attend a public gay meeting by himself. I was curious too. A whole new world was about to open up to me.

Motive, *1972 (Artwork: Kenneth Pitchford)*

Mike Yarr, with sign, out and proud in 1971. (Photo: David Aiken)

Nancy Tucker, shown here in the 1980s, let GLF men know that their behavior and language offended her. (Photo courtesy Kathleen Buckalew)

CHAPTER 2

Argument and Purpose at GLF Meetings

"SUCK." It took one word—and fully a year after the 1969 Stonewall riots—to kickstart Gay Liberation Front in Washington.[1] It took two other words—"women" and "blacks"—to give GLF its perpetual challenge.

After Stonewall, the homosexual world changed in an instant as gays left a repressed era and entered an enlightened one—at least, that's the impression many people have about this watershed. But even among homosexuals, things didn't happen quite so fast, and definitely not smoothly. Although within two weeks of the Stonewall disturbances the radical Gay Liberation Front of New York began to meet,[2] many gay people outside New York City were unaware that this confrontation at a Greenwich Village bar had even occurred. In the pre-Internet world of 1969, the news typically spread, by today's standards, glacially, person to person. Many gay people—myself included—remained in the dark.

Homophile activists who had been working quietly for civil rights for years found out pretty fast that life would not continue as it had. (The term "homophile," which ignored the sex in "homosexual" and emphasized love instead, was about to be displaced by the blunt, three-letter "gay," which for a few years applied to both men and women before "lesbian" demanded equal footing.) One week after Stonewall—at the fifth annual Reminder Day demonstration (reminding the public that homosexuals did not have full civil rights) staged in Philadelphia by homophile groups including the Mattachine Society of Washington[3]—a change was evident. "There was this buzzing in the air," said one MSW member. Demonstrators ignored the organization's strict dress rules, came in jeans.[4] And in a display of affection unimaginable under Frank Kameny's "respectable" homophile approach, one lesbian couple walked hand in hand, whereupon he, affronted, tried to separate them.[5]

As GLF groups began forming, not just in major cities but also in smaller cities and college towns, groups such as Mattachine suddenly seemed stodgy and out of step. In late August 1969, radicals who had shown up uninvited at the national convention of the North American Conference of Homophile Organizations in Kansas City, Missouri, rejected "appeals to 'respectability' "[6] as a way of advancing the cause of homosexuals. They laid out much of the liberation rhetoric to come: Oppressed gays are linked to other minorities, such as blacks, women, Hispanics, Indians, hippies, youth, students and workers. The enemies of oppressed peoples are a repressive governmental system, organized religion, business and medicine.[7]

Gay liberation would invigorate sexual politics in D.C., if a group would only get started! But, despite GLF firing up around the country, nobody started anything in the federal city, not yet. When it finally formed, D.C.'s Gay Liberation Front attracted a crowd that began loudly to unload all their complaints about the straight world, and about one another, including about the white men who assumed leadership. But amid the noise, the group did manage to establish purposes and confront the way gay bars discriminated against their own.

WHY DIDN'T GAY LIBERATION Front form in Washington soon after Stonewall? In 1969, as many as 250,000 homosexuals lived in the metropolitan area,[8] a population clearly large enough to support a radical gay group. But on the street, things were better than they had been, and the police seemed to have given up the 1950s practice of vice raids. The head of the D.C. Police morals squad stated in 1969 that male homosexual arrests totaled 69 in 1968, down from 496 in 1960.[9] Still, many local gay civil servants were vulnerable to job loss. So, an unobtrusive routine of bars and parties was the lifestyle choice for many gay people. No need to invite trouble.

But a new generation of gays with little to lose was ready for change of some kind, and one of them, Michael Yarr, acted. He saw an article in the June 9, 1970, local underground newspaper *Quicksilver Times*, that brought him up short. It was headlined "Suharto Sucks."

Yarr, a D.C. native and a former Young Republican, had revised his political views upon his release from the Air Force in January 1970.

He enrolled at George Mason College (later a university), turned hippie and got involved in antiwar politics. While attending a Black Panther rally in New Haven, Connecticut,[10] with four friends from a group called Northern Virginia Resistance, Yarr saw a notice for a Gay Liberation Front workshop and experienced a moment of self-recognition. Those three words instantly told him all he needed to know. "I went, 'Oh my God.' Here it was. ...I did cartwheels inside." He would attend.[11]

Yarr recalled the workshop as "a spiritual experience." Fifty or 60 people were there, "a lot of Gay Liberation Front people from New York. ...After a few hours they...asked, 'Is this the first meeting for anybody here? Their first gay liberation experience?' I raised my hand and in my halting way said, 'I'm overwhelmed. I've been a self-acknowledged homosexual but had just one sexual experience as a kid. This is probably the most wonderful day of my life.' " After the meeting he told his antiwar friends "what I'd been doing, how wonderful it was, how I felt. Everybody was really supportive."

When Yarr saw the "Sucks" headline about the authoritarian president of Indonesia, he was struck by the insensitivity of the language "We took a lot of instruction and guidance from the women's movement, and we were conscious of sexist language," Yarr said. In today's social media world, any politically insensitive posting might receive a wave of invective from online readers, and fast. In 1970, an angry Yarr expressed his opinion by writing and mailing a letter to the editors of *Quicksilver Times*, which they published in the June 9, 1970, issue:

Sisters and Brothers,
In the last issue of Quicksilver, you ran an article on Suharto of Indonesia. The headline was "Suharto Sucks" and that use of the word suck was blatantly oppressive to gay brothers.

That Suharto is a fascist pig-friend of Amerikan imperialism is right on, but when you equate his fascism with sucking cocks, you put yourselves in the camp of the pig oppressors. Sucking cocks is neither ugly nor unnatural, but rather a sexual expression used by many people.

...Inadvertent slurs against gay people such as "Suharto Sucks" within the "liberation movement" point out the neces-

sity in Washington for gay radicals, militants and revolutionaries to get our shit together. We must "Seize the Time." ...All
Power to the People
    Gay Power to Gay People

Yarr got enough positive responses to his letter that planning for a
Gay Liberation Front meeting space began. Then local writer and activist David Aiken wrote a more fleshed-out call for establishing GLF in the
June 23 *Quicksilver*. In his article, Aiken pointed to the most basic need
of gay self-respect: "It's no surprise that the 'straight world' expresses
its dread of homosexual feelings with repressive tactics. What is really
tragic, however, is that those who experience these feelings accept the
prevalent notion that they are...dirty, evil, and sinful, and repress themselves. So that's where Gay Lib comes in, folks."[12]

A final inspiration was provided by the First Christopher Street Liberation Day and Gay Pride Week (June 22-28, 1970) in New York.[13]
Several men who were soon to start GLF-DC went to the event and were
swept up in the excitement of a political movement that had exploded
there. As one man recalled: "I had an epiphany...that it was really OK
to be gay...that there was something special and unique about being
gay, and that it wasn't necessarily something that I had to hide."[14] At
the end of a week of seminars, workshops and dances, the weather was
perfect for a huge liberation march to Central Park.[15] People were giddy
with elation, proud, strong. Gays held hands, embraced and kissed in a
10-block-long procession filled with banners and signs.[16]

Still, the young movement was not a unified family. Within this joy-
ous throng, a number of identity groups were evident. To name a few: the
black and Puerto Rican Marxist group Third World Gay Revolution;[17]
Gay Youth; the Marxist cell group Red Butterfly;[18] Fems Against Sexism
(males who felt dominated by more masculine males); and Radicalesbians (women who mostly severed ties with GLF and men in general).[19]

BACK IN D.C., flyers posted around town listed the time and place of
the first Washington meeting: June 30 in the parish hall of Grace Episcopal Church in Georgetown. Grace sat serenely a block from the clamor-

The parish hall at Grace Episcopal Church in Georgetown, site of GLF meetings for several months in 1970-71. (Photo: Steve Behrens)

ous intersection of Wisconsin and M. The old stone church overlooked a wide grassy expanse that fell away toward the C&O Canal, all in all an almost rural spot suitable for contemplation in the middle of a busy city. Not a bad place to begin a revolution.

Around 40 people came. Some of them had undoubtedly paused in front of the church and wondered, should I cross over from the safety of anonymity to the danger of publicly acknowledged homosexuality? They undoubtedly had excuses at the ready if they happened to run into someone they knew—I stumbled in here by mistake, I'm doing socio-logical research.

Inside, the attendees were a mixture of long-haired counterculture "freaks," conservatively dressed office workers, a few flamboyantly ef-feminate young men, even some butch bikers. Some had been in the life for years and acted as if they had nothing to lose;[20] others were hesitantly starting to identify as gay. They were mostly white, male and young. A few black men came, plus a handful of Latinos. About a quarter of the group were women.[21] Adding to this cauldron of intersecting identities were older people, Jewish people, the obese, even the blind. Some Mat-tachine Society members were there, curious about this new energy in gay politics.[22]

For three hours, the men and women sat in a circle of folding chairs. Simply by being in a lighted, public room, in a meeting advertised as "gay," they had made a radical choice. They were ready to be seen and heard. They were now GLFers, and a small new community.

And so now what? As discussion began, some in the room began to release years of pent-up anger and hurt. Emotions poured out in long meetings week after week. A jumble of issues emerged:

The bars don't want hippie freaks as customers. I feel discriminated against. Plus, bars are exploitative "meat racks." We need an alternative to the bar scene, some other way to meet people.

I got fired from my job as a waiter in a Georgetown restaurant for wearing blue nail polish. Let's picket.

The Groovy Guy contest *[a small-scale imitation of the Miss America beauty pageant, in which participating bars would parade their contestants in casual clothes and bathing suits]*[23] is sexist and objectifying! We should organize against it. NO, the contest is a meaningless diversion. Let's talk about something serious.[24]

The police are hounding us on "the Block." *[Plainclothesmen were increasingly observed driving around this popular cruising area around 31st and Dumbarton streets in the middle of residential Georgetown, then inviting pedestrians into their cars and arresting them,[25] often on vague charges.]*[26] We are doing nothing but quietly strolling around one square block of Dumbarton Street five or 10 times a night—we're not criminals, we're helping keep Henry and Nancy Kissinger's house safe![27]

We need to stop camping and using demeaning terms like "queen" and "Miss Thing."[28] They are relics of history now that we are openly gay. NO, exaggerated effeminate behavior and camp humor free you from the old proscriptions against anything that does not fit the defined masculine role. Being obvious helps identify you as a radical gay. Besides, street transvestites were among those who fought back at Stonewall, so queens became our first martyrs.

If anyone deserves condemnation, it's the "closet queens." Open and proud gays must condemn gays who pretend to be straight, people like married men who have gay sex secretly. This behavior denies the truth of who an individual is and involves others in a lie. NO, closet queens need our help in accepting who they really are.

Talk kept circling back to the most basic issue: oppression. Everyone agreed that gays had been physically attacked, psychologically pressured to conform, tossed out of homes, outlawed, fired from jobs, deemed sick (even subjected to institutionalization, sterilization, castration, lobotomies, and more),[29] and called sinners. How should we respond? Do we defiantly let others know that we won't tolerate mistreatment? Or do we calmly educate the public and stress the ways we are not so different from them? The underlying issue—are we radicals or liberals?—was never fully resolved in GLF, and arguments on some variant of this went on week after week in general meetings.

The radical line said, As an oppressed people, we need to align ourselves with other oppressed peoples to end injustice wherever it occurs. Many GLFers had been active in the civil rights and antiwar movements, and some in women's liberation, and they made a logical leap to gay liberation. As one participant said, "We didn't see a difference between fighting for the rights of any minority that we identified with and fighting for gay and lesbian rights."[30] The black rights and women's movements could help advise the gay liberationists. In fact, representatives of the Black Panther Party and Washington Women's Liberation spoke in general GLF meetings.

The liberals and moderates argued that we can't solve every problem in society at once. We can't end the war in Vietnam, for instance, or discrimination against blacks. We welcome everyone to join us, but we're not here to align with other groups. We need to concentrate on gay rights. When we act, we should take well-planned actions aimed at achievable results. We want a reasonable, orderly, nonviolent approach to change, including outreach to straights.

Over the weeks, as the group settled into two basic camps, general meetings became heated discussions, with people vying to establish the

unassailably correct high ground. And even basic organizational structure was debated. "Most of the members are liberals and desire some sort
of organization," the GLF Newsletter reported in September 1970, "but
time and time again the radicals put any type of organization down."[31]

It was raucous, exhilarating, frustrating, boring. As one participant
put it: "Madness, chaos, anarchy. Everybody had an opinion and they
were all wrong and I was right."[32] Tom Shales, later the TV critic for the
Washington Post, reported on the group for the *D.C. Gazette*. In spring
1971, the members were still going at it: "There was constant stress
between radical, liberal, moderate and semi-conservative elements of
the group. Worse, there was a continuing game of what's-my-guilt? being played. One person would accuse another of racism and himself be
accused of classism. ...some obviously could not decide under which
manifestation they were most oppressed—as blacks, or as gays, or as
women, or as black gay women, or what."[33]

IN THE BEGINNING, GLF was adamantly unbureaucratic,[34] and so
was not really an organization at all but a kind of "anti-organization."
The group had no president or any other officers. Anyone who attended
could call himself or herself a member. Decisions were made by consensus, which often took a long time to reach. "They just met, and that
was it," said one attendee who found the meetings delightfully full of
hippie rebelliousness, and "nearly ideal" in their flexibility and loose
structure—but at the same time stressful. "I would more often than not
leave the GLF meetings very frustrated because we just ended another
evening with just a lot of talking," he said.[35]

Not a great deal got decided, but those who wanted to establish some
basic goals did succeed. Within a few weeks, the attendees managed to
come up with a few nonradical purposes for the group: (1) to establish
a sense of community among gay people, (2) self-knowledge, and (3)
education of the straight community.[36] GLF also created committees.
The word "committee" seemed too organizational to young radicals, so
the made-up word "glonk" was substituted for "committee"[37] and, thank
heaven, abandoned not long after. Committees were formed for political action, communications (a newsletter was soon being published),

social events, fundraising and new member orientation. Even a steering committee was added to try to impose agendas on the gatherings[38]— with times specified for business, general rap, and special workshops or speakers.[39]

Frank Kameny was often in attendance, providing information and suggesting actions. Many GLFers respected him for his achievements and expertise. But to others, especially young veterans of student radical politics, he seemed too authoritarian. Could this intimidating, singularly unfashionable, slightly shabby 45-year-old with his barking voice even *be* gay? One attendee recalled that Kameny "dressed in a suit and tie every goddamn day. He showed up at GLF, and here were all these hippies. They weren't going to listen to him. Plus of course Frank is very commanding with his booming voice. You know, 'Do it my way or don't do it at all.' And of course they just said, 'Fuck you.' "[40]

Kameny engaged as best he could with the unruly but remained firm in his sense of what needed to be done to advance gay rights. I imagine that he viewed these young radicals with some combination of suspicion, distaste, attraction, impatience and hope—hope that they would come around to appreciating all the progress he had carefully achieved, hope that he could combine the excited energy of GLF with the organized discipline of the Mattachine Society. Opportunities for appropriate actions did present themselves from time to time. One involved D.C.'s sodomy law,[41] which imposed severe punishments for those convicted of the crime. He had long wanted to challenge the law, and now he orchestrated a case against it. First he needed volunteer plaintiffs. He later recalled that, at an early GLF meeting in 1970, when he called for "people who were willing to put their names on a list, to say that they engage in sodomy under certain conditions, that they violate the law...there was almost completely a deafening silence."[42] But in fact, at least three of the four male plaintiffs who signed up for the case were GLF attendees.

ONE OF THESE WAS Richard Schaefers, who had been involved in the liberationist politics emerging at Columbia University before moving to D.C. in 1968. Despite his college activism, he was fearful about entering gay life in Washington—he had to force himself to go into gay bars but could only get as far as pretending to use the pay phone before fleeing. Finally, at the Georgetown Grill, for the first time, "I noticed that no one had two heads, so I stayed."[43]

Schaefers later said he basically wanted to use GLF to come out. But he also volunteered to be a plaintiff in the sodomy case. On Aug. 21, 1970, Schaefers wrote a guileless letter to Inspector Walter Bishop, director of the Metropolitan Police Department Morals Division, inquiring: "I would like to know whether any provisions of the laws of the District of Columbia make it a crime for two adults of the same sex to live together in a homosexual relationship, engaging in homosexual acts, including oral and anal intercourse, in the privacy of their home."[44] Hmm?

Inspector Bishop wrote back, politely assuring Schaefers that such "unnatural and perverted" acts were serious crimes.[45] Indeed, D.C. law penalized those convicted of sodomy with a $1,000 fine or 10 years' imprisonment.[46] Once the case against the D.C. chief of police and the director of the police morals division was filed in U.S. district court in September 1971, Schaefers's contribution was essentially complete (and he didn't have to demonstrate any unnatural acts).

By the end of May 1972, the law was declared invalid: Homosexual acts between consenting adults in private were no longer subject to criminal prosecution.[47] Presiding judge Charles Halleck also found the law against soliciting an unconstitutional invasion of privacy.[48] The *Gay Blade* announced that "verbal proposals made to persons 16 years of age or older, no matter how explicit, for private, consensual sexual acts are now legal in D.C. unless the speaker persists to the annoyance, disturbance or offense of the unwilling stranger."[49] (This issue was far from resolved. In 1974 the D.C. Court of Appeals overturned Halleck's ruling about solicitation for sodomy.[50] In 1993 the D.C. Council repealed the District's sodomy law,[51] and Congress did not interfere, as it had done in 1981.)

"I was a drone," Schaefers later said. But the drone had gone public when called upon. Very public. The *Washington Post*, in reporting on the suit, included not only his name, as he expected, but his employer's name as well.[52] Fortunately, that understanding employer was Arena Stage, where Schaefers spent his career and eventually became business manager.

HOWEVER MESSY AND UNSTRUCTURED, GLF meetings could be exciting to attend, and they attracted more and more people. For some, giddy joy mixed with relief at finding someplace they could be themselves. The potential for political change was palpable, as was the potential for romance. And despite the emotions and the confusion, a sense of personal wholeness could emerge for some who were there. As one GLFer assessed the group: "You could go to a meeting and shout at each other all night, and yes, practically nothing got accomplished, except something happened to your spirit. Something made you feel strong."[53] Gay people were tearing up the script they had been handed and writing a new one. Even though isolated homosexual protests had taken place elsewhere long before Stonewall, as far as D.C. GLFers knew, they were in the forefront of a new era of history, making history. Another activist described the excitement: "Every night I didn't want to go to bed because I felt if I did I would be missing something."[54]

After the very first GLF meeting, several elated young men and women walked up Wisconsin Avenue to get a drink at the Georgetown Grill, the neighborhood gay bar. The now-revolutionary brothers and sisters were ready to decompress a bit and discuss what they'd just experienced. But their excitement vanished when one in the party, a woman, was refused service. In this men's bar the presence of a female customer was a problem. The group identified themselves as gay—just to make sure the waitress knew they weren't straight freaks who'd wandered in by mistake—to no avail.[55] The waitress would not serve the woman. So much for gay liberation (and women's solidarity) in gay Washington.

The next night an outraged group of about six men and two women from GLF came back determined to be served. One man in the party recalled the Grill waitress, who was well known to Washington gay men: "She was wonderful if you were a gay man and tipped her. But she didn't like us because we looked nasty and had women with us, which was an abomination at the Grill. She first carded them—not us—and they had IDs, so then she announced she could not serve them because they were wearing slacks. We had just been through this revolutionary hoop-de-do, and we weren't going to take that. So we said, 'We're having a sit-in until you serve them!' "[56]

Whatever the waitress's impression, these radicals clearly stood out

Above: Undated photo of the Georgetown Grill from the Facebook page of Preserving LGBT Sites in Metro DC. *Below: the site in 2020, after a 2006 redevelopment kept only the zinc-coated facade. (Photo: Steve Behrens)*

amid the sport shirts, tight chinos and neat haircuts of the men in the bar. (As he told me in 1994, long-haired GLFer Bruce Pennington had had a similar reception at the Grill in 1968: "My first experience of hospitality in a gay bar was: 'Beat it. We don't serve hippies.' ")[57] The group's sit-in lasted about 15 minutes, as the protester recalled, "and then a cop walked in, which dampened everyone's spirits, including all the gay men in the bar." He talked to the protesters, then to the waitress, who apparently told the police they had caused trouble the night before.[58] Then they "came back to us and told us we had 10 minutes to get out of there. We all scampered away like mice. But we had had our first action. At least we'd spoken up and shown solidarity with women."[59] The Georgetown Grill had just served up the latest case of discrimination against gays—by gay bars—and given GLF its main cause.

The local gay bars' practice of excluding customers they deemed undesirable—sometimes subtly, sometimes blatantly—was nothing new. In the post-World War II period, some men's bars denied entry to women. As for African Americans, even after 1953 when restaurants were required by law to serve blacks, businesses found ways to avoid serving them. Some restaurants would place "reserved" signs on tables so they could tell blacks wishing to be seated that no space was available.[60] In 1970, "inappropriate" dress and "insufficient" proof of age were two means of making sure those unwelcome at bars got the message.

GLF's first order of business at the second weekly meeting was responding to the outrageous denial of service by the Grill. Some attendees wanted to picket the bar, and an ACLU lawsuit was considered, but everyone finally agreed on a more measured approach: Send a general letter to a range of D.C. gay bar owners requesting an informal meeting to talk about the problem of discrimination.

Since the case was about denial of civil rights, Frank Kameny, an authority on such things, jumped in to help. He worked with GLF members to draft the letter, had it typed on Mattachine letterhead, and signed it "for the Gay Liberation Front, the Homophile Social League, the Mattachine Society of Washington." The August 1970 letter stated in part, "That a person should be refused service because he is black or she is a woman, is not only illegal, but is paradoxical to our striving for better human understanding. Unfortunately, we have noted that several of you apply these considerations in a non-uniform and discriminatory fashion for the camouflaged purpose of excluding certain groups."[61]

Three weeks passed, and the only bar to respond was the 1832 Club on Columbia Road NW, which was known as a place where people of different backgrounds mixed.[62] A second letter went out. No response.[63]

By November, many men wanted direct confrontation of the bars.[64] One man dramatically suggested just burning the "mothers" down—to general laughter. Others wondered whether confrontation would be effective. Someone suggested that discrimination would continue as long as gay bar patrons desired it, that "bar owners are going to cater to the wishes of the bar spenders."[65] With no consensus about how to proceed, GLF shelved further action for the moment. But the group had at least established its position; it would revisit the issue later.

MEANWHILE, DESPITE THE earnest group effort to prevent discrimination against women, women began to desert GLF as their sensitivity to oppression as women, not just as gays, began to assert intself.

The women's movement was burgeoning before Stonewall, and women had made strides with consciousness-raising groups, actions and theoretical writings. In GLF-DC, politically experienced women were meeting men who grew up in the age of *Leave It to Beaver*, when little more was expected of women than cooking for and cleaning up after their boys. Now, that attitude was no longer tolerable to women.

A group of women staged a walkout of the Aug. 25 meeting, declaring their aim to organize a women's group to be allied with GLF but not part of it. "Hopefully," the GLF Newsletter ventured, "the split will be only temporary so that the *girls can get their heads together*." [my italics] Efforts were made to keep women involved. As one of its first decisions, the GLF commune at 1620 S St. NW scheduled a Sunday women's group.[66] Representatives of Washington Women's Liberation spoke at one general meeting.[67] But by the end of 1970, only two women continued to attend GLF meetings.[68]

In some ways this disappearing act reflected arguments going on nationwide among feminists. Many lesbians had been active but invisible in the women's liberation movement since the mid-1960s, when Betty Friedan's *The Feminine Mystique* stirred many American women to political awareness. But the issue of lesbians in the movement changed after Stonewall, when many lesbians became involved in GLF. In May 1970, at the Second Congress to Unite Women in New York, a group of women who had been active in GLF, including writer Rita Mae Brown, distributed copies of a "manifesto" titled "The Woman Identified Woman" and wore T-shirts announcing (and appropriating Friedan's negative description), "Lavender Menace." Among the Radicalesbian manifesto's pronouncements: "A lesbian is the rage of all women condensed to the point of explosion." And, "Lesbian is a label invented by the Man to throw at any woman who dares to be his equal."[69]

Suddenly, lesbianism in the women's movement was undeniable, and many lesbians active in both women's and gay liberation found themselves pulled in opposite directions. Feminists, straight or gay, put pressure on them to commit to the cause of women rather than the cause of men. Feminists would say that gay men are just like straight men: rapist mentality, etc. Sometimes the lesbians would push back: "This is still our movement. You straight feminists are ashamed to be seen with us." The feminists would counter, "You seem to be ashamed of admitting that you're women. You want to stand with gay boys and be fag-hags."[70] And so on.

Feminists who had also been active in male-dominated antiwar groups such as Students for a Democratic Society repeated the familiar complaint that they were assigned to fix coffee while the boys planned and then went off on their activist adventures. Coffee was not served in GLF-DC. What was served was a lack of equality and respect.

The women's complaints surprised some men, who then acknowledged their own sexism and declared their support of women. "I was probably a typical oblivious man," said one. "All of a sudden the women expressed their complaint that men dominated, and I had never thought of it before then. And the men certainly did dominate. Anybody could speak up at a meeting, and everybody would shout."[71] And there was (perhaps unconscious) physical jockeying for dominance going on, with prime spots in meetings taken by men. The GLF Newsletter wrote that in meetings men were "always chairing and doing most of the talking" but insisted that men needed help from women to overcome their chauvinistic attitudes.[72]

A few men resented women with a chip on their shoulder, or women who didn't understand gay male culture, or women who didn't explain exactly what was offending them. As one man said, "We were supposed to figure out what it was that we were doing that was oppressing them. It was impossible. Nobody knew where to begin."[73] But then, as one woman said, she was not interested in educating "chauvinist pigs" and raising their level of consciousness.[74] Men would have to figure it out on their own.

The Gay Blade

October 1969   Vol. 1, No. 1
An Independent Publication Serving the Gay Community

BLOOD DRIVE LAUNCHED	Is the gov't run-	GAY LIBERATION FRONT
The need for blood is crucial. Do help! Members and supporters of Mattachine are participating in a Red Cross blood donor program.	ning a security check on you? Being black-mailed? Need draft counseling? Call Franklin Kameny, president of the Matta-chine Society of Wash-ington at 363-3881 for	After raids on the Stonewall bar and the usual police harass-ment, the NYC gay com-munity has formed the Gay Liberation Front. First to feel its in-fluence was the Vil-
Give blood in the		

Nancy Tucker was coeditor of what later would become the Washington Blade.

NANCY TUCKER, FIRST coeditor of the *Gay Blade*, and the self-described "last woman standing" at GLF meetings, had her own griev-ances, which she finally proclaimed loud and clear. Politically, Tucker was an individualist. She later termed herself simply "gay." She "was never a part of the women's movement, was never a member of any organization like the Furies or NOW."[75] Yet she was very sensitive on the issue of respect for women. Around April 1971,[76] Tucker took her leave of GLF for good, reading a "white-hot" farewell statement titled "Fuck You, 'Brothers'" at a general meeting. In it she listed the misogynistic offenses committed by the men, offenses that had apparently been sim-mering in her for months.

Born in 1946, Tucker began to feel the need for some gay friends when she was about 20, but she hardly knew where to begin. How do you find gay people? At a newsstand at 15th and F streets NW that sold "adult" magazines, she found gay publications from San Francisco. Reading them, she discovered that there was a Mattachine Society quiet-ly operating right here in Washington. To assure her privacy, she called the MSW number from a pay phone near her parents' home in Northern Virginia. Following Mattachine rules, she waited until she was 21 to join. She went to the MSW office on F Street to be interviewed by Frank Kameny and two others. Her impression was that they were concerned that she might be a government agent.

Once accepted, Tucker began attending Mattachine meetings, which were held in a windowless basement room behind the furnace in a Capitol Hill church.[77] Up to 25 men and women came. After two years in MSW, she dropped out. Later, she was asked, along with Bart Wenger, to produce a one-page mimeographed newsletter Mattachine was putting together, the *Gay Blade*.[78] (As the *Washington Blade*, the country's oldest LGBTQ newspaper, it is still publishing.) When GLF started in 1970, she attended meetings as both an interested gay person and a *Gay Blade* reporter.

In her farewell letter to GLF-DC, Tucker wrote that she was leaving because:

> ...this organization and this movement offer me nothing. Why should I be interested in homosexual rights—they're based on (male) homosexual problems: entrapment, police harassment, blackmail, tea room assignations, venereal diseases. Christ, I can't relate to that kind of shit; it has no meaning whatsoever for me.

"Whatever sex predominates or can get the upper hand in conversation is the sex that will be heard most of the time," Tucker recalled in 2014, "and their concerns are addressed most of the time. I've learned this in the last 40 years, just from experience, and it exasperates me now as it exasperated me then. And of course exasperation was what we were supposed to do then. We were supposed to be annoyed. We were out to try to change the world."[79]

> I'm leaving because I'm disgusted. I can't relate to people (read that men) who need people (read that fetish objects). Snow queens, dinge queens, chicken queens, muscle queens, queen queens... Pick your favorite, or add your own to the list. I see this fetish thing in every male homosexual I know. I don't see it in women. Thank God WE see people as people, not as objects.
>
> I can't even withdraw into homophile literature without being offended. Naked "studs" on every page. And those ads! "Wanted—triple amputee for photo exchange." "Want cauc. Male, over 8 inches, for Greek pleasures." "Black stud needed as master for willing white slave." And on and on, *ad nauseam*. The ads abound with fetishism. Whatever happened to *people*, huh?
>
> I'm sick of watching skag drags parading up and down,

prancing and dancing in their "finery" and mocking me and my sex with every step. I'm tired of hearing somebody referred to as "Miss" when he's done a no-no: "Miss Terry, well she's always late." "Miss Chuck, she can't seem to get herself together..."

Tucker later said that camping and "skag drag"—men wearing women's clothing in public without any attempt to hide the fact that they were men—were common at general meetings. "So here were these august discussions of equality and applying feminism to the gay movement, and so forth. And yet there were these subtle put-downs of the entire female sex going on at the same time."[80] (Incidentally, the world of formal drag organizations and drag entertainment were apparently exempt from feminist criticism; news of drag events was ever present, without editorial comment, in the *Gay Blade*.)

> I'm tired of being called "girl." I ceased being a "girl" several years ago. I am on my own now, I support myself, and I conduct myself in an adult manner—I deserve to be called a woman, and I have many more claims on that title than many of you do to the appellation "man."

Tucker recalled that at meetings men would repeatedly use phrases such as "men and girls," and almost automatically, she "would pop up with the word 'women'! ...And a little later it would be 'girls,' and I would pop up, 'Women.' I got tired of that. ...So I would be loudly saying the word 'women' so that everybody in the room could hear and hopefully learn. And it seemed that they didn't."[81] Instead of saying, "Oops, sorry," upon being corrected, some men couldn't seem to remember to use "women," or wouldn't. One of the offenders was Kameny. Because he was older and seemed "out of touch with modern-day thinking," recalled one activist, "he'd slip and use the word 'girl,' and all hell would break loose."[82]

But then again, Tucker herself had used the word "girl" a few times in the early *Gay Blade*.[83] That was before her own "sudden enlightenment" on linguistic correctness when, after a women's meeting, another woman there pointedly referred to her as a "woman." "I remember the shock that went through me, being called a *woman*," she said.[84]

> You faggots, and I use that word with every ounce of malice I possess, could care less about women. And you will suffer for it.
>
> Every time you put down a woman, you drive the knife just that much deeper into your own gut. You are committing suicide by your depreciation of the opposite sex.
>
> Gay Liberation will never succeed until Women's Liberation succeeds. Your fate hinges on that of women, like it or not. Male homosexuals will not be equal until women are equal.
>
> Liberation? Gay Liberation? Liberate yourselves, my friends. For myself, I don't need you or it.

"I worked myself up, definitely," Tucker recalled. "I did not go back and edit it six days later in order to take out any nastiness. ...I know I was angry. Really, really angry."[85] Still, despite her rage, Tucker remained friends with some men in GLF and continued to be involved in gay causes.

One participant remembered that the diatribe and walkout had little effect on the men.[86] After a brief period of stunned silence, they presumably engaged in guilt-ridden discussion, then went back to the arguments du jour.

Tucker later said that gay men and lesbians worked together again only after the AIDS epidemic struck.[87] She left the *Gay Blade* in 1973. In 1979, Tucker helped found what is now NALGAP, the National Association of Lesbian, Gay, Bisexual, Transgender Addiction Professionals and Their Allies. She later settled in Albuquerque, New Mexico.

IN MAJORITY-BLACK Washington, Gay Liberation Front was a majority-white organization; that was obvious at a glance. The question was, how to attract African Americans to gay liberation?

Many black gay Washingtonians would have known about GLF meetings because, almost from its start in 1969, the *Gay Blade* was delivered to some black bars. But black gays could have had a number of reasons for not attending public gay meetings. Black gays may have seen GLF as a white group that had little understanding of the everyday problems of the District's black residents, which included restricted housing, discrimination in employment, lack of education and poor health care. By 1970, the earnest Kumbaya days of the early-'60s white-supported civil rights movement were gone, and many who had then identified as Negro now called themselves black. Two years after the assassination of Martin Luther King Jr. and the resulting Washington riots, and with the Black Panthers and other separatist movements going strong, black Washingtonians may have felt little desire to associate with whites for any reason.

"Another factor that kept African-American lesbians, gay men, and bisexuals rooted in the black community was the significance of familial ties," wrote Genny Beemyn in *A Queer Capital*. "White gay people typically left their families to pursue same-sex sexual relationships. ...Because black lesbians, gay men, and bisexuals often remained in or near the Washington neighborhoods in which they were raised, they lived out their sexual lives within the confines of their home communities, making it difficult to conceal their same-sex sexual desires from families and friends."[88]

With racial segregation a fact of life in Washington, the city developed two separate gay social scenes. An informal network of African American social clubs expanded in the 1960s. Typical get-togethers were private parties and potlucks. Soon more formally organized social clubs proliferated. Clubs such as The Group, the Pinochle Club and the Metropolitan Capitolites held dances, competitions, fundraisers for medical research, and celebrations of members of the black community.[89] The Metropolitan Capitolites later started their own bars—the Zodiac Den, the Third World and the ClubHouse.[90]

The clubs also had historical precedent, according to Will O'Bryan, writing in *Metro Weekly*: "One reason for the clubs—which one could argue go back as far as the black, gay salons of the Harlem Renaissance in New York or earlier 1920s gatherings in Washington that included Langston Hughes, Bruce Nugent, Angelina Weld Grimké and other rising stars of the African-American GLBT universe—was an uneasy, covert chasm between black and white gays in D.C."[91] In the white bars, with their overly strict carding of blacks, "you just felt like you weren't welcome," said Otis "Buddy" Sutson, who cofounded the club the Best of Washington. "We were never thrown out of any establishments or anything like that. It just felt cold. It wasn't a warm environment."[92]

Black gay Washingtonians' response to this exclusion was apparently less about demanding equal access to places where they felt unwelcome and more about creating their own social world. Expressing mixed feelings about D.C.'s racial divide, Sutson said:

> I think our [black] culture is different, and I think we have to embrace that. ...I used to be a big proponent of integration in a sense. But integration is a double-edged sword. When you integrate, you lose some of the good things that you have: your own little communities, your institutions, what really makes you click. There has to be a balance, but I don't think integration has to be the total goal.[93]

The social clubs, then, existed primarily to provide a comfortable environment and a good time for members, many of whom remained closeted at home and work. According to Sutson, virtually none of his friends were involved in sexual politics.[94] Later, in the 1980s, when AIDS devastated the social club community, some clubs stepped up with support services for those living with AIDS.[95]

Within GLF, some minority attendees began to express their frustrations in general meetings. In December 1970, they announced they wanted to meet separately from the whites. "Third world people are fed up," one said, "with the white male chauvinism which dominates the gay movement." There was some dismay about this possible walkout, considering the exodus of women, but the need to work things out as a separate group was acknowledged.[96] Whether a minority caucus formed or the idea fizzled is unclear, but there was at least one reason why some minority attendees stuck with GLF: Several blacks and Latinos were housemates with their white brothers in the GLF commune, which may have given them pause before an angry walkout.

Conflicts in general meetings were still going strong in June 1971, and gender and race were only two of the possible topics. Reporter Tom

Shales described "a continuing game of what's-my-guilt" at general meetings, with accusations of racism and classism volleying back and forth.[97] Some conflicts were absurd. One attendee, Shales wrote, "older than many, was continually castigated because he wore a hairpiece. It came to symbolize his bourgeois capitulation to the straight world, apparently; he had a respectable job, that sort of thing. The issue of his toupee kept coming up until one week it came off—he tore the thing from his head and threw it on the floor."[98] Now he was liberated and the criticism would stop!

Observing "all this soul flogging," Kameny offered his own take-it-or-leave-it opinion: "The door was open…in good faith, to anybody who happened to come along. …And if it ends up being white, middle-class, then fine. That's the problem not of the people who were there, that's the problem of the people who chose not to be there."[99] (The Mattachine Society had earlier handed out MSW literature at black bars in Washington, with little response.)

There is no evidence that GLFers, white or black, took any concrete steps to attract more black Washingtonians to meetings, though discussion continued. The upside of perpetual talk about gender and race was the opportunity for attendees to consider their own attitudes. Ultimately, outside forces prodded GLFers to act. One thing was clear: Someone else's discriminatory treatment of women and minorities was outrageous. The bad guys were the bars, not themselves.

THE GEORGETOWN GRILL protest had gone nowhere, but in mid-January 1971 the Plus One bar on Eighth Street SE was discriminating. Reports circulated that the upscale bar made it difficult for blacks, women, drags and unconventionally dressed people (meaning counter-culture "freaks") to gain entry. One gay newspaper reported that "they don't want you if you're not white, middle class and straight looking … The manager claimed he wasn't aware of any discrimination, but he did admit that the bar wanted to maintain its butch, Ivy League image."[100]

On-and-off picketing took place for a few weeks, and finally the bar's co-owner, Henry Hecht, met with GLF representatives. He explained that asking for two IDs and refusing admittance to women, drags and those

GLF picketers confront the Lost and Found in 1971. "Well, you can't please everyone," bar managers captioned this picture. (Photo: Lost and Found)

under 21 was an attempt to stay within the law and avoid trouble renewing its liquor license. This despite the fact that beer could be sold legally to 18-year-olds. And drags were excluded because drag was illegal, according to the Plus One; but drag *was* legal in D.C. The end result was a victory, sort of: Hecht agreed to post a nondiscrimination statement near the bar entrance, and also to spell out the bar's ID policy.[101]

A messier brouhaha took place months after the Plus One confrontation. The brand-new superbar Lost and Found, owned by life partners Donn Culver and Bill Bickford (who had parterned with Hecht to open the Plus One), boasted a large dance floor with a DJ booth, closed-circuit television,[102] a working fireplace, a light show and a "rain curtain," according to the *Gay Blade*.[103] Located off South Capitol Street in a desolate corner of D.C. that became home to several gay establishments and was near largely black neighborhoods, the L&F had not been open long when word got around that it was keeping some people out. This time protesters took to the streets in force.

Picketers set up shop in front of the bar, and there were a few bruises. Activist Eva Freund was one casualty. She was picketing when she decided to see for herself what the patrons inside looked like. She was admitted, but then someone recognized her as a protester. After refusing to leave, she was tossed out the door by a bouncer and two other men,[104] landing against a parked car.[105] The Rev. Reggie Haynes of the Community of the Love of Christ, which was located at the GLF commune, was also shoved out the door. In response, the little religious denomination celebrated Mass in front of the bar and presumably prayed for the forgiveness of bar management's sins.[106]

Manager Bill Perry was apparently caught off guard by the picketers. He met with activists on Oct. 15, 1971, and, according to them, was bluntly defiant. Perry was quoted as saying, "Black people are generally poor, and, besides, most of our patrons are bigots." He explained that the L&F could not afford to cater to any patrons "who spend only $2.25 a night in our bar."[107] As to the L&F's relationship to the Washington gay community, the bar's management said that "its reason for existence is the profit motive, best served by catering to rich, white, male suburbanites."[108]

In a flyer issued a week later, GLFer David Aiken attacked the Lost and Found's "flagrant discrimination against gay blacks and women." Blue jeans were acceptable for men but not for women; blacks had to show two pieces of identification such as driver's license or birth certificate.[109] Men with long hair also faced alleged discrimination.[110] Picketers demanded a uniform I.D. policy and compliance with the alcohol laws of D.C.[111] "We will not allow them to realize extravagant profits at the expense of the human dignity and freedom of certain gay people," stated the flyer, signed by 19 organizations in the expanding gay community, including the Mattachine Society, Gay Activists Alliance, Skyline Faggots, Gay Women's Open House, GLF, and Metropolitan Community Church.[112]

The Lost and Found issued its own statement denying discrimination and detailing its strict ID policy.[113] Finally, a truce of sorts was reached. A November 1971 L&F publication stated:

> During the past four weekends you have witnessed an effort by certain groups within the "community" to change the admission policies of Lost and Found. Without consulting the Management, they embarked on a campaign of picketing and harassment...we were finally contacted by a representative of one of the moderate factions...it was agreed there had been a

lack of communication, thus causing the misconceptions about our policies...We apologize for the inconvenience, as well as the verbal garbage you were forced to hear spewed from the mouths of the pickets as you tried to exercise your right of freedom of choice. Thank you for your support and consequent rebuttal of this small band of radicals who claimed to be the "representatives and moral guardians for the community."...[114]

It appeared, however, that the protesters had effected some change: In April 1972 the L&F announced that it wouldn't discriminate, except against drags.[115] (This sole exclusion was still illegal.) But in late 1973, reports that the bar was again discriminating against blacks and women led to a personal investigation by *Gay Blade* editor "Patricia Kolar" (a pseudonym for Pat Price). Kolar reported that a bar employee told her that it was "not our policy to serve women at this [middle] bar because the fellows don't want women around here."[116] Owner Donn Culver asserted that Kolar had a personal vendetta against the Lost and Found and said that the *Gay Blade* would no longer be distributed at the bar. By the end of the year, the bar issued a statement that all customers would be served there.[117] The L&F closed in 1991,[118] and the entire warehouse/gay club area was later redeveloped.

BACK AT THE GEORGETOWN Grill, which had denied service to female GLFers in June 1970, the world quietly inched forward. After the fruitless letter-writing campaign and the threat of a lawsuit—and probably because of actions at other bars—change came. Within a couple of years, the Grill gave in to progress and began serving women.

With my housemates Rick, left, and Jennifer in Potrero Hill, San Francisco, 1970.
(Author photo)

CHAPTER 3

A Breather on the Coast

IN THE SUMMER OF 1970, needing to escape Washington and start anew somewhere else, I moved to San Francisco. I sold or gave away most of my possessions—black leather sofa, white cube tables. I even blithely let my grandfather's antique oak rolltop desk go for $40, my car for $150. I stashed my semi-feral cat Sadie with a friend. That left only what I could stagger around under in a backpack—including a sleeping bag and an autoharp, which I spent more time tuning than playing. Free at last of everything!

After the cross-country road trip, I arrived alone in San Francisco on August 7 and spent my first night in a Black Panther crash pad, where I learned that the Marin County courthouse shootout—in which four people including a trial judge were killed when a 17-year-old tried to force the release of "Soledad Brother" George Jackson—had taken place that day. I didn't sleep well.

After about two weeks in various crash pads, I looked up a friend of a friend in the Potrero Hill neighborhood. Rick was an artist; he lived with Jennifer, a boyish lesbian with a long blond braid down her back, plus a dog, and Faith, the sole survivor of a litter of three kittens. Every day, we three got up whenever, threw the Ching for guidance about the day ahead, listened to the Stones' *Let It Bleed* album, considered what to do about lunch or dinner, and tried to stay stoned. Typically, we visited friends in the neighborhood—David was a gourmet cook; Nicholas was a dark, bearded ascetic living in a tiny hillside house filled with hand-crafted objects; Carol was a speed freak; Georgia was an older lesbian who owned hundreds of Billie Holiday recordings—or we made day trips in someone's car.

While I was living in parasitic indolence in San Francisco, GLF-DC was in its prime, so I missed about three months of D.C. life.

Then in October 1970 my vulnerable diva Janis Joplin died, and I sank into a depression and then a homesickness. The flower child trip was over, and I flew back to D.C. at the end of October. Still collecting unemployment, I moved into a group house of straight men at 18th and S streets for a while. If I wasn't fascinated enough to attend GLF meetings, I was fascinated by the gay life that had developed around the GLF commune, two blocks away, and considered the men there my friends.

One night, a week before Christmas 1970, I was curled up in my tiny room when one of my straight housemates told me someone was asking for me at the front door. Out on the sidewalk a group of men from the GLF commune were caroling for my benefit. They had combined an outing to distribute GLF literature with Yuletide tradition. For someone away from home—and most of us were—it was a heartwarming gesture.

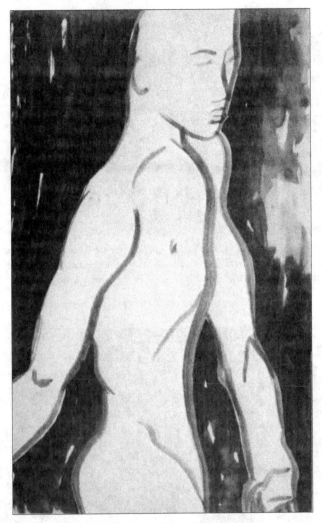

Motive, *1972 (Artwork: Kenneth Pitchford)*

The GLF House in Dupont Circle was political home for some, crash pad or community center for others. David Aiken (first row, second from left) and Bruce Pennington (first row, right) with housemates at the commune on S Street. (Photo: Rainbow History Project)

Residents of a very, very, very gay house celebrate Gay Pride in New York. (Photo: David Duty)

CHAPTER 4

Inside the GLF Commune

THE FRONT DOOR WAS USUALLY OPEN. In 1970, you just walked into the house at 1620 S St. NW, at the sketchy eastern edge of Dupont Circle. Visitors were coming and going all the time, and it was obvious that the young people who lived there had nothing much to steal, so during the day at least there was little point in locking it.

The house stood only a few blocks from 14th and U, the starting point of burning and looting after the assassination of Martin Luther King Jr. in 1968. Two years later, the ravaged 14th Street corridor had little to offer its now even worse-off residents, and junkies often hung out in the area waiting for "the Candyman."[1] Muggings were an occasional fact of life on S Street, and most of the young white people who lived in the neighborhood gravitated west to the stores and restaurants of tony Connecticut Avenue, six blocks and a world away from 14th Street.

Inside the 1879 townhouse[2] were elegant high ceilings, fireplaces and pocket doors. But 1620 S also exhibited a scuffed-up weariness, in part because it had already served as a commune. The previous occupants were antiwar activists connected to the draft-resisting priests Daniel and Philip Berrigan.[3]

When it became a Gay Liberation Front commune (often called the GLF House), the household was much like the 40 or so other communes scattered around Dupont Circle, Adams-Morgan, Mount Pleasant and Capitol Hill:[4] threadbare furniture, posters and thrift-store art on the walls, cheap curtains on the windows, "liberated" signs, a misbehaving cat, political flyers, messages taped to the refrigerator. Except this was a household whose purpose was proclaimed by the handmade banner in the living room: "D.C. GLF." As far as anyone knew, the idea of radical gays living communally and openly had never been tried before in Washington.

On most any day, passing through the entry hall to the living room, you entered Grand Central Gaydom: People were gathering for meetings. Men were parading about in thrift-store dresses. Someone was on the phone giving information about gay liberation, or advising a runaway teenager, or taking calls from another GLF group needing a place to stay in D.C., or even dispensing information on venereal disease.[5] There might be spontaneous dancing. And if you were looking for something to do, maybe you could join a group of soon-to-be-ex-strangers heading out somewhere. If you happened to go upstairs, you might find some bedrooms cheaply decorated, others with just a mattress on the floor, a dresser, clothes strewn about, and maybe a record player; a closed door usually meant that two men had quietly slipped away hand in hand to be alone. Downstairs was a large basement usable for meetings or overflow guests, or just for hanging out. And everywhere was the smell of cigarette smoke, and often the pungent scent of marijuana.

Within a few weeks of its start in June 1970, Washington's Gay Liberation Front was starting to fulfill two of its stated purposes—"to establish a sense of community among gay people" and "self-knowledge."[6] Perhaps the founders intuited that the need to unify and support gays preceded any more high-flying goals, such as ending oppression everywhere. When a group of gays rented the house, "we were going to create a community, and we are going to work things out," as original member Bruce Pennington recalled.[7] So they set about creating the locus for radical gay life and forming consciousness-raising groups to foster personal growth.

ON SEPT. 1, 1970, five white men, one Puerto Rican man and one African American woman moved in. Most had at least part-time jobs, so they were able to swing the rent of about $250.[8] Two of the original residents emerged as key forces in the household.

Writer and editor David Aiken is generally acknowledged to be a quiet leader or—perhaps more accurately—facilitator of the commune. David himself later expressed his reticence about leadership, suggesting that a pitfall to avoid is "any organization in which people compete for titles such as president or chairman, and in which the winner of such contests is duly acclaimed as 'leader'...it's the very macho 'leadership' attitude that many of these people demonstrate that we must combat before wars will end." [9] Despite the rhetoric, he was always ready to help answer questions and gently guide others if asked. A tall, skinny man with dark hair and nerdy Coke-bottle glasses, David attended the University of Chicago and arrived in D.C. in 1968 as a reporter for the *Chicago Sun-Times* but later worked as an editor for the Joint Center for Political Studies.[10] He had a patient, logical approach to consensus building that was enriched by wide-ranging intellectual interests and a quirky sense of humor.[11]

Bruce Pennington, on the other hand, was wildly theatrical, especially when inhabited by his radical alter ego, "Aurora Borealis," complete with feather boa, granny glasses, long sideburns and drooping mustache.[12] He combined a laissez faire, free-spirited attitude toward communal life— drugs, sex and rock 'n' roll—with a take-charge seriousness, especially when dealing with outsiders such as journalists or possible government informants.[13] Bruce grew up in North Dakota. Inspired by the civil rights and antiwar movements (and a need to get out of Rugby), he arrived in D.C. at 21 in 1968 to join the leftist Liberation News Service. He did not stay long at LNS, and during the rest of his life worked mainly as a waiter, a chef and a D.C. charter school teacher. To activist Nancy Tucker, Bruce was sharp and funny. "And because I thought he had some brains behind all his noisiness and bravado, I respected him."[14]

Despite their contrasting styles, Pennington and Aiken worked well together, and they later helped found and run the local gay radio program *Friends* and, in the 1980s, the D.C. chapter of Black and White Men Together.[15] Aiken helped form the Washington Area Gay Community Council, a coalition of local gay groups and businesses.[16] In the late 1970s, Pennington became a licensed foster parent to a gay adolescent and successfully defended his custody when the boy's parents challenged his fitness in court.[17] He was a founding member of the Rainbow History Project, which archives and promotes the history of LGBTQ Washington.

The one woman resident at 1620 had just spoken at a women's rally at Farragut Square in August, putting forth the case for militant lesbianism and disparaging male supremacy.[18] In the commune, it was soon clear that she was a resident only. She spent most of her time in her room and did not eat communally with the men.[19] Whatever good vibes existed in September evaporated. One day a group of women arrived at the house and moved her out, to the relief of all.[20]

Despite the end of the mixed-sex household and the hand-wringing in general GLF meetings about the group's inability to attract many African Americans, the commune was always solidly multicultural. Members were committed to interracial living, and nearly half the residents were minorities at some point.

In addition to the permanent residents, a steady stream of back-pack-laden young gays in town for antiwar rallies and protests often found a place to stay at the GLF commune. A nationwide network of radical gay groups was well established by 1970, and GLF-DC had a reputation as a sort of national capital crash pad. The house also took in gay teenagers kicked out by parents, desperate for guidance and a place to stay. "We…gave them a bed to sleep in, made sure they were in clean clothes, helped some of them get jobs," recalled Pennington.[21] The household soon began to grow, since a casual invitation to put someone up for a few days might turn into an additional permanent resident after a couple of weeks.

Still, the open-door policy extended only so far. Occasionally, a visitor might fall under suspicion as a possible government infiltrator or a narcotics agent looking for criminal or subversive activity. The always-protective Bruce remembered a tall, blond man in well-polished shoes visiting the commune and seeking information on how to become a drag queen.[22] Bruce suspected he was a police officer, questioned him closely and finally told him to leave.[23] And there were enough odd clicks on the phone to assume the line was being tapped, which in the "enemies list" era of Richard Nixon and J. Edgar Hoover seemed entirely reasonable.

The residents agreed on house rules: They would share rent and food expenses as well as divvy up the cleaning chores; they would regularly prepare and eat meals together; and they would meet regularly to reach basic decisions and address any problems that might arise. Just as in the chaotic general GLF meetings, house meetings at 1620 could be a challenge to decision-making. But David usually was able to guide the residents toward consensus.[24] If it sometimes seemed that using "correct political process" to decide who did the dishes was overkill,[25] still the residents generally respected the decisions. Life on S Street could be emotionally rewarding, especially at mealtime, with its sense of familial togetherness. But the group also reflected the larger counterculture in their dedication to having a high old time and using grass or acid as often as possible. Bruce recalled that "our first Thanksgiving the turkey was stuffed with dope."[26]

This casual approach, in which the bourgeois virtues of cleanliness and order were minimally observed, worked for the most part. Still, living in the commune was a major adjustment for some. Seemingly blissed-out "Moonbeam" (Paul Bartels), a suburban 18-year-old with thick, dark hair falling down his back, was "desperate to come out" and leapt at the opportunity to move into the house when there was an opening. But once there, he discovered that living in D.C. required money, and he had none. And there were roaches! He came to realize that he was used to a clean, orderly life. Finally, after two weeks, when he noticed that people weren't putting his LPs back in their sleeves, that was enough. Not quite ready for full-time communal life, he moved back in with his understanding parents and eased back into the life by spending weekends at the commune.[27]

SINCE THE COMMUNE LISTED itself in the District telephone book as "Gay Liberation Front," calls seeking information and advice would come in day and night. And 1620 S was soon hosting meetings of every kind. According to Pennington, activities often came about through a "visceral" sense of need. For example, "there was a need for people to have a coming-out group, so we announced one, and people came."[28] Political meetings, rap (discussion) groups—including a women's group[29] and a mixed rap group[30]—consciousness-raising sessions, left-wing lectures by outsiders were all held at the house.[31]

1620 S St. NW, location of the GLF commune (Photo: Steve Behrens)

The spacious basement was used for introductory sessions on gay liberation. In some cases, people hesitant about coming out might get a nudge of encouragement.

The GLF commune also provided a social space, an alternative to the streets and the bars. After the June 1969 disturbances at the Mafia-owned[32] Stonewall Inn in New York, bars were regarded by gay radicals as politically incorrect places—dark, dirty, out-of-the-way dives where men approached each other only as sex objects. The radical answer to the bar "problem" was to create a relaxed setting where people could meet and relate as human beings. The commune hosted casual open-house events. GLF founding member Mike Yarr met Billy Bradley in October 1970 at a newcomers open house there. Billy had already noticed Mike when one day he saw a group of three or four men walking through the park between P and M streets, holding hands. As Mike recalled, Billy said, "I noticed you then and I got this feeling of jealousy of how happy you all looked." When they met at the get-together, Mike was instantly attracted to Billy but tried to be cool about his interest. He did tell Billy that he worked at Discount Books, and two days later Billy showed up at the Connecticut Avenue bookstore. Soon thereafter they were a couple.[33]

Parties were de rigueur at the commune. Any excuse to celebrate—birthdays, Halloween, rent money—would do, and the floor sometimes trembled under the dancing.[34] At a birthday party in 1970 for resident Michael Ferri, with not much more provisions than punch and music, some exotic guests appeared: parents! Michael's father and stepmother came. Despite the generational and lifestyle gap, the couple mixed easily with the young radicals. Then a black Dupont Circle queen named Princess—who had a marcelled upsweep and the hauteur of a diva—arrived in a white fur stole and spent time happily chatting with Michael's father.[35] The birthday cake was in the shape of male genitals, Michael recalled, so he emasculated it and declared, "Down with male supremacy!"[36]

After meetings and other activities, people often ended up at the S Street house to unwind and extend the togetherness. One after-party at the commune[37] followed a dance at St. Mark's Episcopal Church in Capitol Hill.[38] GLF, along with the Homophile Social League and the Mattachine Society, sponsored the Nov. 14, 1970, dance. Almost 200 people attended—myself included—and a live band provided music. (The congregation had already replaced pews with chairs to create an adaptable space, so the dance was held in the cleared sanctuary.) To me, even a sedate foxtrot in the cavernous, chilly sanctuary, with the altar looming in the darkness, felt like some church social gone rogue. But most others leapt into the spirit of the event with abandon, and inevitably, a circle formed that involved a mass of "writhing, dancing sisters and brothers" experiencing "fantastically good vibrations."[39]

Picnics were another popular activity. An August 1970 picnic in Fort Reno Park, in the Tenleytown area, attracted about 70 people in 91-degree heat. Highlights included a spontaneous halftime conga line at a straight soccer game. After some teenagers started calling the picnickers names, the gays held an impromptu teach-in. All in all, a success: "A grand time was had by all and everyone was able to find the place very easily...they could smell the Aramis for miles!"[40]

CROSS-DRESSING WAS encouraged at the GLF commune. The group took the position that liberated people had the obligation to live honestly and openly. As a result, some men spent time exploring their "feminine side" in activities that in their earlier lives had been absolutely verboten except on Halloween. Men who as boys had suppressed any interest in "girl stuff" could now abandon all reservations.

Formal drag had long existed in Washington, of course, and since the early '60s the Washington Academy had provided structured activities and safe venues for cross-dressers.[41] But drag as practiced in the world of liberation was not about verisimilitude or entertainment but about politics. For radicals, drag challenged traditional gender roles. The GLF message about dress and behavior was: Be gay, look gay, act gay, the gayer the better. It was OK to embrace a "sissy persona," or carry a purse, or call everyone Miss Thing.[42] Many men even took to kissing other gay men, *on the mouth*, as a way of greeting them on the street. This at a time when, as one participant recalled, even holding hands in public was "a tremendous affront to straight people. They can't handle it...to be affectionate in public is really crossing the line."[43] But shaking hands does not a revolution make.

A writer in Berkeley's underground paper *Gay Sunshine* declared in October 1970 that "blatant is beautiful." Any effort on the part of gays to blend in and "pass" as straight in order to avoid oppression was inexcusable. "Dressing straight" to appear more desirable, he wrote, is "like saying Straight is Good and Gay is Bad."[44] And drags had been the first to resist police harassment at Stonewall, so drags had an honored place in the movement, at least on paper.

The radical form of cross dressing, "skag drag," took drag aggressively beyond camp. A man doing skag drag (aka gender fuck) wore women's clothing in public without any attempt to look like a real woman. Today this form of cross-dressing is a common sight at Pride celebrations, but in 1970 skag drag was a rare, boldly radical statement. With skag drag, the answer to the question "Do we confront the straight world with our radical homosexuality?" was *Yes*. Don't like it? Get over it! It was easy to put together a skag-drag look. Just assemble thrift-store fashions from the 1940s and '50s, old costume jewelry (rhinestones preferred), pillbox hats, silk milliner flowers, add lipstick and mascara, whatever—and voila. A few examples:

"Flambé" (Wade Carey) explored makeup and dresses at the GLF commune to perfect his look. The feathers and lace he wore in public were radically gay but also artistic. He used his skinny height of well over 6 feet, long red hair and clean-shaven face to advantage, and recalled feeling proud of being a "flaming creature." He gravitated toward bright colors, tie-dyes, yellow knee boots and Chinese dressing gowns.[45]

Activist John Scagliotti joined a group of hairy-legged men in high heels "with beards and lipstick and hippie beads," and walked to the White House to "celebrate" first daughter Tricia Nixon's wedding in June 1971. He had never before done drag and didn't foresee the difficulties of walking in a miniskirt and high heels the distance from S Street to Pennsylvania Avenue. "By the time we got there, everybody's feet were sore...but we looked great."[46]

"Total Assault" (Jim Fouratt) was a slight man with little-boy-lost blue eyes, but he was formidable in skag drag. He once stalked down edgy 17th Street in a black dress, pearls, beard and combat boots, invincibly self-confident. His version of street theater—confrontational, ridiculous—was a "gender-free" statement in reaction to the rigidity and restrictiveness of traditional masculine and feminine roles. It was, in brief, an effort to achieve "total change in society" by living the revolution[47]—a Total Assault on the status quo of male behavior.

But skag drag ran up against women's sensitivity to any form of misogyny. Despite the idea of liberating men and women from traditional roles, many feminists were offended by campy behavior and cross-dressing among men, perceiving them as hostile, demeaning parodies of women. But even after denunciations of drag and camp at GLF meetings, the practices persisted.

EVEN I TENDED TO THINK of some gay men as irresponsible, immature hippies, not as the complex, often sober individuals many of them were. One example of their commitment to something other than politics, sex and drugs was the creation of a gay church at the GLF commune. Despite GLFers' sometimes careless, dismissive attitude toward the congregations that granted them meeting space, and their anger toward official church positions on homosexuality, many in GLF still had spiritual needs that wanted expression. In fact, even at the first GLF meeting, a sampling of ex-Roman Catholic seminarians happened to discover their common background when someone got up and said, "If anyone's been in a Roman Catholic seminary, please meet in the corner to talk"—and several men convened.[48]

In September 1971, a few men living at the commune started the Community of the Love of Christ. They dubbed the living room the Chapel of St. Francis and St. John.[49] Later the chapel was set up in the roomier basement.[50] Anyone was welcome, and even straight neighbors sometimes attended.[51]

Gay religious activity had been stirring across the country for several years. The Rev. Troy Perry started the Metropolitan Community Church in Los Angeles in 1968,[52] and a local ex-seminarian, Paul Breton, started the D.C. congregation in May 1971. In New York, the Church of the Beloved Disciple (started in 1970) emphasized formal ritual and welcoming gays. Another influence in the movement was political gadfly Mikhail Itkin, who led churches of various names and supported gay liberation, pacifism, civil rights and the ordination of women.[53] In July

1972, Itkin ordained two men (Joseph Covert and Reggie Haynes) living in the GLF commune as priests in the Community of the Love of Christ.[54]

The Community, with its emphasis on Mass form, was loosely similar to what one might encounter in a Roman Catholic or Episcopal church. And as MCC's Breton recalled, politics was always implicit in this church. "It was not impossible to combine Marxist ideology with Catholic ideology."[55]

Joe Covert and others led services in a chapel at the GLF commune. (Photo courtesy Rainbow History Project)

The GLF commune chapel scheduled an ambitious lineup of regular worship services, often with guitar accompaniment:[56] two Masses every Sunday, one on Wednesday, plus prayer services, even a midnight rock-folk-soul Mass.[57] In 1972, Holy Week culminated in an Easter Sunday celebration featuring music from the musicals *Jesus Christ Superstar* and *Godspell*.[58] The little denomination lasted only into 1973. It apparently dissolved when the group house on S Street broke up that year.[59]

WHAT DO YOU LIKE TO DO IN BED? How do you get along with your parents? What frightens you about being gay?

By late 1970 I had ventured upstairs at the commune, to Theodore Kirkland's bedroom, where my consciousness-raising group was tentatively answering questions about sex and feelings. Men didn't do this sort of thing easily, but Billy Bradley, Steve Behrens, Steve Lindenbaum, Theodore—he was always "Ted" to me—and I were making a go of it.

Based on a model used mainly in the women's movement, consciousness-raising groups were small groups, separate from general GLF meetings, in which members committed to meeting for a number of weeks to discuss issues facing them. Also known as cell groups, CR groups were meant to "raise the consciousness" of members by helping them understand external oppression, so that they could better respond to it, and also to examine their own internalized oppression in the form of fears and hang-ups[60] so that they might become more confident and self-accepting. Everyone was encouraged to join a group; volunteers would even line you up with one.[61]

CR group discussion depended entirely on members' interests. Discussion could be free-form or structured around a specific topic. Pressures to conform, coming out, gay bars, sexual experiences with women, feelings about effeminacy, masturbation, family life[62]—all were typical topics in meetings. Groups sometimes explored sexism, racism or class shame.

Many found CR groups to be positive experiences. One man felt so liberated from being in a group that he came out "in every aspect of my life."[63] Another man recalled being in the Army, quietly living with a lover and associating with a group of gay Army buddies—but never actually discussing what being gay meant. When he later joined a GLF cell group, he said, "If there was a moment when I came out, it was that time, finally accepting what was going on with me."[64] Another man had been appalled at the cutting viciousness of many men he met in bars. It was not until he joined a GLF CR group that he realized gay people "are just normal people. And that was a great relief to me."[65] Sometimes members wept as they recalled growing up as "sissy boys" and suppressing their natural behavior to conform to social standards, and now for the first time getting positive feedback for such behavior.[66] At least one group moved toward specific political action.

An influential document in consciousness raising was Carl Wittman's essay "A Gay Manifesto" (1969), photocopies of which were handed out at early GLF meetings. Wittman, a San Francisco antiwar activist who had come out publicly in 1968,[67] described the symptoms of internalized oppression: lack of self-respect, self-censorship, self-hatred, shame and accepting the status quo. He wrote, "Our first job is to free ourselves; that means clearing our heads of the garbage that's been poured into them."[68]

His vision of liberation was prescriptive at times. He declared certain sexual practices to be anti-gay perversions. Things like seeking only heterosexual partners and wanting to be a "top" but never a "bottom" were examples of "role playing at its worst," he wrote. "We strive for democratic, mutual, reciprocal sex." But running through his provocative essay is Wittman's ideal of the love and support that gays could now provide one another, and a new definition of who gays were: "Homosexuality is the capacity to love someone of the same sex."[69] The new message was that gay people did not represent a lack of heterosexuality or a failure or error of any kind. This was an affirmative new way to think about being gay.

Steve Behrens quietly acted on the principles of gay liberation. (Photo: Steve Behrens)

My group mostly concentrated on sharing life stories. One of the things we discussed was coming out. Steve Behrens grew up in Arlington, Virginia. As a teenager struggling with his sexuality, he heard that there was a gay bar in Georgetown; he looked for the Georgetown Grill but never was able to find it (and was too embarrassed to ask). He did manage to read a magazine article about the "curse" of homosexuality, and he couldn't identify himself with the horrible condition he read about. Ultimately he came to accept that he was gay. In his senior year at American University he came out to his roommate.

Being honest with others about your sexuality was central to gay liberation, in part because it opened the door to changing others' opinions and behavior. Steve's roommate admitted to being gay as well, and Steve then discovered that several of his college friends were gay.[70] Even romantic relationships had quietly formed. Several of the men started going to GLF meetings.

Steve later decided to make the simplest and hardest statement a gay person can make to those closest to him, "I am gay." As he later recalled:

> I've been lucky with my parents. They were accepting, although they were not happy about it. ...I left them a note rather than having a confrontation in person. When I came back

later that night, my father was sitting in the living room, in a grumpy mood. At some point he told me this little story:

When he was a boy living in the Seattle area, he had a job on one of the steamers that went from town to town on Puget Sound. And on a steamer one of the other crewmen once approached him, grabbed him or something, propositioned him. And he said, "I wanted to break his arm." So he was basically telling me that he had had very negative feelings about homosexuals. ....[71]

Steve's father told him to go see his mother. "I'm sure that she was very sad," Behrens recalled. "And one of the first things that came to mind for her was the fact that she might never have grandchildren. And another thing that I think comes to mind for a lot of parents of gay kids is that they have done something wrong. I think that worried her a lot. ...But my parents came around."[72] Steve, an editor and photographer, later cofounded the biweekly newspaper of public TV and radio, *Current*.

CR groups were not for everyone. One man recalled being kicked out of his group for being shallow and not in touch with his inner feelings. The members were sharing their guilt about being homosexual, and he didn't have any.[73] Others found all this touchy-feely sharing a waste of time when action was called for. Frank Kameny considered consciousness-raising "one of the things that bogged GLF down endlessly...I thought it was excellent for those people who were still buying into the attitudes of bygone eras."[74] But although Frank may have had the steely conviction to leave old attitudes behind, many others were still timidly emerging from a lifetime of indoctrination. And Frank's own compatriots in the Mattachine Society had struggled in 1965 to agree to a statement that homosexuality was not an illness—but only after great debate and some unconvinced leaders saying that "we're really all mentally ill."[75]

The topic of CR groups was debated in general GLF meetings. As one GLF Newsletter put it, some proponents of consciousness-raising groups "seem to feel that little worthwhile can be accomplished by GLF until the feelings of members can be heightened to a certain degree," and that activists are "jumping the gun." The activists wanted demonstra-

My cell group (Theodore Kirkland, nonmember Michael Ferri, Steve Lindenbaum, Billy Bradley and myself) in Harper's Ferry, W. Va. (Photo: Steve Behrens)

tions, marches and confrontations now, and accused others of not doing anything.[76]

But the five of us in Ted's bedroom bought into consciousness raising. Week after week, we sprawled on his bed or sat on the floor, fumbling forward in our do-it-yourself psychotherapy. We shared ourselves seriously and immediately got respect and support in return. For me, being with other men in a consciousness-raising group was the opposite of my experience seeing a silent Baltimore psychologist. My CR group was the key experience of GLF for me, the heart of being part of a community. Here the good news of Stonewall finally reached me—that I was the way I was supposed to be. As a writer for *Gay Sunshine* put it, CR groups "may well be the most profound development in our movement."[77]

LIKE MOST OTHER communes, the GLF household ultimately broke up. Overcrowding was a major factor, especially with overextended visits, and money was tight. One long-time guest recalled, "I don't know how I lived for a year without any money…I never had unemployment, I never went without food."[78] With more mouths to feed, it became harder to come up with the rent and buy food. For a time, spaghetti became the basic shared meal several nights a week.[79] Bruce recalled that sometimes "people kept food on the windowsill, because if they kept it in the refrigerator it would disappear."[80]

After formal GLF meetings were ended in summer 1971, house members vowed to continue the work of GLF. By April 1972 the commune called itself the Gay Lib Services House, held regular meetings and planned to continue providing a 24-hour-a-day information switchboard, a library of gay materials and a counseling center.[81] But gradually, key residents moved out. Michael and Ted left in 1971, fed up with the overcrowding and weary of supporting freeloaders. A burned-out Bruce moved out that fall.[82] David left. Somewhere along the way the commune became simply a bunch of gay guys sharing space with no pretense of communal living. By the end of 1973 the owner of the house wanted the property back, so the experiment was over. The center of the gay community disbanded, though most of its activities—organizing, educating, counseling—continued elsewhere.

Despite all the craziness, every once in a while, the house was also a calm oasis of just being together with "family." One GLFer remembered a visit to the commune in 1971:

> One Sunday night I walked into the house. It was summertime and warm; the house was open. Nobody on the first floor. I yelled upstairs: No one was on the second floor. And from downstairs I heard this gorgeous song. It was Elton John's "Your Song." I'd never heard Elton before then...They were all downstairs listening to that.[83]

And you can tell everybody this is your song...

Tom Ashe, shown in San Francisco in the early 1970s, faced incarceration for his belief in gay liberation. (Photo courtesy Richard Lewis)

Chicago "leftie" lawyer Renee Hanover, shown in New York in 1975, came to Washington to defend the D.C. 12. (Photo courtesy Nancy Hanover)

Huey Newton, 1968. (Photo: Blair Stapp/Collection of the Smithsonian National Museum of African American History and Culture)

CHAPTER 5

Action!

ARE YOU A HOMOSEXUAL?
So asked a flyer that Gay Liberation Front members handed out on D.C. streets in October 1970. Those who read past the question were immediately reassured that they were probably not.

> But according to the Kinsey Report, millions and millions of Americans are. The person who gave you this handbill is homosexual.
>
> Take a look. We're human. We're fed up with being called sick, neurotic and "unnatural." We're tired of being confused with criminals and child-molesters. We are average human beings who live intelligent and often creative lives. We believe we have a right to love in our own way.
>
> Nonetheless, homosexual people are feared and viciously discriminated against in employment, in military life, in social and family life, and in the media, all these injustices sanctioned by law. Our way of love, and the fact that we even exist, are considered too shocking to talk or even think about...
>
> Gay Liberation is dedicated to fighting for fair treatment for homosexual men and women, to spreading knowledge of what homosexuality truly is, to opposing discriminating laws and regulations, and to winning for homosexual men and women decent employment rights. Gay Liberation is here today because we refuse to remain silent any longer. We are determined to win the right to a free, open, loving life.
>
> The Gay Revolution Is Here to Stay. Gay Is Good.
>
> Signed: Gay Liberation Front, Homophile Social League, Mattachine Society[1]

Soon after GLF started up in June 1970, attendees decided on three purposes for the group. One of them was "education of the straight community."[2] From the start, then, along with the revolutionary rhetoric, GLF took some traditional, "nice" approaches to reaching people. But over the next five months actions became nastier, and even violent. A second GLF action hurled curses at the Roman Catholic Church and psychiatry. In the third action, GLF joined with the Black Panthers in an effort to rewrite the U.S. Constitution, and a brawl that broke out during the gathering led to a significant case involving gay defendants.

THE "ARE YOU A HOMOSEXUAL?" action had clear objectives and an opportunity to make quotable public declarations, and so was a perfect fit for homophile activist Frank Kameny. With its call for understanding and civil rights, and signed as it was by two homophile organizations, the handout had his fingerprints all over it. It even juxtaposed "Gay Revolution" and Kameny's trademark "Gay Is Good." (Participation in the Panther gathering, with its broad New Left aims, was too diffuse and idealistic in objectives to interest Kameny.)

The flyer distribution—taking place in the downtown shopping district and in Georgetown, Capitol Hill and Dupont Circle[3]—would be GLF's first planned contact with the straight world, and some of the young volunteers were nervous about public exposure.[4] And what if they were arrested? This was a realistic concern—on at least one occasion, men distributing gay literature were arrested for littering.[5] But Kameny, an expert on the rights of gays, would be available to help deal with any legal problems resulting from the distribution of materials.[6] "Are You a Homosexual?" went off without incident. The volunteers handed out nearly 6,000 leaflets,[7] and reaction was about one-third hostile, one-third sympathetic and one-third indifferent. One young woman said, "Are you kidding? There's a shortage of guys as it is."[8]

DR. JOHN R. CAVANAGH was just settling into his lecture, "Latent Homosexuality as a Cause of Marital Discord," in McMahon Hall at the Catholic University of America. A psychiatrist and longtime lecturer in

Catholic University's McMahon Hall was the site of a 1970 zap aimed at psychiatry and the Church. (Photo: Steve Behrens)

the CUA School of Sacred Theology,[9] Cavanagh had organized a week-long November 1970 conference on religion and the homosexual.[10] He was droning on about anxiety and psychological impotence and Canon Law...[11]

"Bullshit!"

This comment came not from any of the 40 to 50 priests, nuns and ministers who were there,[12] nor from the theology students who got credit for attending.[13] It came from an angry-eyed young man who had quietly entered the hall along with about 35 others, and the man's companions took up the call. Cavanagh was being zapped by the Gay Liberation Front.

John Cavanagh was something of an expert on homosexuality. It's clear from his 1966 book *Counseling the Invert*, which recounts much of the established psychological and religious commentary on homosexuality, that Cavanagh was at least sympathetic to the problems homosexuals faced. He was aware of organizations such as the Mattachine Society and their demands for civil rights for gays. He was also aware of more radical issues that had bubbled up earlier among homophile groups, such as the right to marry and to adopt children.[14] He even had a sense of humor, at least on the subject of marriage. He once criticized the "rhythm" method of birth control, drolly musing that the experiences of his patients "made me wonder if God intended Catholics to suffer so."[15]

But Cavanagh stood at the intersection of traditional psychiatric and Roman Catholic views on homosexuality. Psychiatry categorized homosexuality, in its *Diagnostic and Statistical Manual*, as a "sociopathic personality disturbance," and the Church labeled it sinful. In *Counseling the Invert*, written for the benefit of pastoral counselors, he asserted that homosexuality "represents a defective development of the personality with a fixation of the libido at an early age of development." He also wrote that homosexuality is "objectively immoral" in that it is opposed to both divine and natural law. Among other attributes, according to Cavanagh, homosexuals are narcissistic and "likely to submerge reason to emotional forces." The goal of a pastoral counselor, he wrote, is to lead a homosexual to a celibate life, to chastity in response to homosexual desires.[16]

Now, a year after Stonewall, an unchaste rabble was here shouting that the church oppressed gays by teaching hatred and superstition, and that psychiatry enforced its preference for heterosexuality through shock treatment.[17] In 1970, even the use of the word "invert" in a book title must have seemed like a red cape waving in front of bullish radicals. These people were clearly not like the more cooperative subjects Cavanagh had researched. Narcissistic? Maybe. Emotional? For sure. Some of the zappers—members of the GLF consciousness-raising group that hatched the idea of the zap—were working their way through a lifetime of Catholic shame and guilt. Others simply wanted to stop the flow of misinformation coming from supposedly authoritative sources. Today they were clearly not inverts; they were *outverts*, out to shut the enemy down.

Deciding to attack had not been easy. Some radicals wanted to take over the entire weeklong conference. Some said crashing the seminar would end it.[18] Some said CUA had no right to hold it anyway. Some worried that a takeover would offend conference participants, and that violence would teach straights nothing. Others argued that violent disruption was the only way to shake "self-complacent straight do-gooders" out of their misconceptions.[19]

Perhaps seeking to move the young radicals to a decision, Kameny, who was an official CUA seminar participant, told them he was planning a seminar takeover on Friday in order to present an all-homosexual program.[20] The younger gays quietly decided on a one-day Wednesday disruption.[21] And so now they had entered the forbidding stone heap of McMahon Hall, not far from the even larger Shrine of the Immaculate Conception, with its gleaming yellow-and-turquoise dome.

As a conference panelist, Kameny was in a position to express his typically incendiary opinions. An atheist, Kameny had no particular stake in Roman Catholic teachings, but he was happy to leap into the fray when theologians were purveying ignorant and harmful information. Early in the week, Kameny addressed the conference and began hurling his firebombs: "How dare you insult us by including homosexuality in such a program with male prostitution, child molestation and behavioral therapy!" and attacking the Roman Catholic Church as a "a sex-obsessed, sex-drenched and sex-saturated institution."[22] And, amid what he called "two days of utterly dismal orthodox psychiatry and orthodox theology," Kameny also sensed that the audience of priests and nuns had become "as fed up in their way as I was in mine."[23]

Although Kameny had announced early in the week that militants had decided *not* to demonstrate against the seminar,[24] now it was Wednesday and a young man was cursing at Cavanagh. Other interlopers took up the chant: "Bullshit! Bullshit!" The moment was difficult even for a few protesters. One "nice ex-Catholic boy," Michael Ferri, felt embarrassed by the cursing,[25] and another former seminarian, Paul Breton, "was really scared to death that day."[26]

The protesters moved toward the stage, where the flustered Cavanagh was trying to continue. Waving a pink flag, they surrounded the academic. It was just not the time for establishment opinions on homosexuality. The protesters took over the podium and nudged Cavanagh aside.[27] Someone tossed Cavanagh's notes in the air. One young man read a statement, mimeographed on pink paper, while others stood behind him, arms around each other's shoulders, and kissing:[28]

> We are homosexuals: As leaders of the Gay Liberation
> Front we deny your right to conduct this seminar.
> 1. We demand that you stop examining our homosexuality
>   and become homosexual yourselves.

2. We do not seek acceptance, tolerance, equality or even entrance into your society with its emphasis on "cock-power" (read male supremacy).

3. We hold the Catholic Church and the institution of psychiatry responsible for political crimes committed against homosexuals such as imprisonment, blackmail, beatings, psychological rape, and loss of economic security. We also feel every gay suicide is a political murder!

Only we as homosexuals can determine from our own experiences what our identity will be—and that will happen in the new society which we will help to build.[29]

Some of the priests and nuns in the audience wanted to hear what the protesters had to say.[30] But this was not a teach-in. The young gays had accomplished their mission. They came down from the stage and paraded around the room chanting "Gay power to the gay people!" and then left.[31]

Cavanagh tried to continue: "Now that we've had our fun, I'd like to resume this statement." But Kameny interrupted, saying, "This will continue happening until you start talking *with* us instead of *about* us!"[32] In a discussion period afterward, the radical tactics were deplored but at least one attendee thought the protesters had good reason for hostility: "Dr. Cavanaugh sees every homosexually oriented person as 'sick' …'selfish.'" With all the problems gay people face, "why burden these brothers and sisters with the label of pathological?"[33] Some attendees wanted to "throw out the rest of Cavanagh's agenda and set the program themselves."[34]

The conference schedule did change. On Thursday, as prearranged, Cavanagh discussed his research on the causes of lesbianism, and long-time activist Lilli Vincenz, who the day before was uncomfortably part of the demonstration, was now calmly offering evidence for Cavanagh as an invited panelist.[35] But Friday was now gay day. The speakers included a gay Catholic priest; a nun who attacked psychiatry and Catholic theology; an Episcopal priest;[36] and David Aiken of GLF.[37]

All in in, the Catholic University zap was a success. Dr. Cavanagh was able to maintain his dignity. About the protest, he sniffed, "These things don't prove anything to me but bad manners."[38] (The director of workshops at CUA later accused the demonstrators of being "hostile to the Catholic Church and professional psychiatry."[39] Well, yes.) On the GLF side, the protesters stopped Cavanagh in his tracks without violence. They got to shout four-letter words and accuse the Church and psychiatry of various crimes, up to and including murder. Kameny got to spew colorful vitriol about two of his longtime bogeymen. Plus, the protest made the newspapers, so gays got some free publicity.

And perhaps best of all, some hearts and minds appeared to change. When the conference was over, some of the activists took about 20 of the attendees out to visit gay bars.[40] Earlier in the week, Kameny had said, "You can learn a lot more in a few hours' tour of Washington's fine gay bars than from all the psychiatrists."[41] So a group of Catholics and gays went out together. Paul Breton, who was one of the protesters, recalled:

> Each of us took charge of about half a dozen priests and nuns...One of the priests who had been at the conference was a great big man, maybe 60 years old. Plump, definitely Irish, ...Smoked a great big cigar. Heterosexual beyond day one. We were sitting in the Plus One. He was in the corner facing out. All of a sudden he puts his cigar down in the ashtray, slams his fist on the table, and says, "I don't see what the hell is wrong with this. They're having fun!"[42]

About a week later, a much different action took place.

TOM ASHE WAS HUNGRY. The 23-year-old had spent all day Friday, Nov. 27, 1970, in meetings mapping out a radical new gay America. Then he'd partied into the evening at a rally in Malcolm X Park, and, along with his boyfriend José Ramos and two others, was headed back to American University to camp out for the night. But the four had to find some food. On Wisconsin Avenue, they noticed the Zephyr, a restaurant-bar near Fessenden Street. It was after midnight[43] and there wasn't much choice. This would do.

On any other night, each man might have made the little behavioral

When four gay men were refused service at the Zephyr, a tavern at this Wisconsin Avenue location, the night in 1970 ended with a brawl and the arrest of 12 gay men. (2014 photo: Steve Behrens)

adjustments that gays in 1970 automatically made when entering an overwhelmingly straight environment. But tonight, camouflage would be a betrayal of all the visions of liberation the four had dancing in their heads. And they were together. Besides, there would have been little point in trying to butch up. José, a somewhat effeminate 18-year-old Afro-Puerto Rican, was wearing a little lipstick[44] and his revolutionary pink beret atop his hair.[45] And he and Tom were holding hands.[46]

The four men—Tom, another white man, José and an African American man[47]—entered the busy Zephyr, a college hangout and sports bar,[48] and sat at a table. While waiting for someone to take their order, two of the men stroked each other's backs and giggled quietly.[49]

After several minutes,[50] a manager approached and told them they would not be served. Later, according to the prosecution, Ramos and Ashe were refused service because they refused to show proof of age, were improperly dressed (José was wearing a sleeveless shirt),[51] and one of them had brought a half-empty bottle of soda into the restaurant.[52]

Ramos put his coat on to cover his shirt,[53] but still no service.

Then, as Ashe recalled, the manager came back with two waiters and said, "We're not going to serve you. You're going to have to leave." Ramos then asked: Was it because of race? There didn't seem to be any other blacks in the restaurant.

"No, it isn't. You'll just have to leave."

"Is it because we're homosexual?" José asked. "Because we're gay?"

"Look, I'm just telling you we're not going to serve you now. You'll have to leave."

"Well, I think you are discriminating against us because we are homosexual, and I'm not going to stand for it. All we want to do is eat."[54]

For a minute, disaster was almost averted when one of the four suggested they order takeout. An incensed Ramos wanted to leave.[55] But Ashe suddenly dug in his heels: "I'm not leaving until I'm served." It was clear to him why they weren't being served, and he felt this was a kind of Rosa Parks moment for gay people. "It was the last time I was ever going to let it happen," he reflected.[56] More words were exchanged; still no service. When the four men stood up to leave, Ramos hurled his most effective weapon: "All right. We're gonna leave, honey, but we'll be back!"[57]

IT WAS ALL COMING together. The Revolutionary People's Constitutional Convention would unite a range of radical groups in support of oppressed peoples everywhere. The Black Panther Party had called the convention because, they said, the existing U.S. Constitution did not go far enough in protecting the rights of the people. According to a Panther handout, it "was written by slave holders to serve the interests of those who oppress black, brown and poor people," and the Panthers asserted that black people "have no future within the present structure of power and authority in the United States under the present Constitution."[58] Radical change was called for: Over three days the delegates from various New Left identity groups would write demands that would then frame a new U.S. Constitution to replace the outmoded one.

The Black Panther Party for Self-Defense had been founded in Oakland, California, in 1966 as a grassroots militia to protect black people from police harassment. It soon formulated a 10-point program of demands:

> We want freedom. We want power to determine the desti-ny of our Black Community.
>
> We want full employment for our people.
>
> We want an end to the robbery by the white man of our Black Community.
>
> We want decent housing, fit for shelter of human beings.
>
> We want education for our people that exposes the true nature of this decadent American society. We want education that teaches us our true history and our role in the present day society.
>
> We want all Black men to be exempt from military ser-vice.
>
> We want an immediate end to POLICE BRUTALITY and MURDER of Black people.
>
> We want freedom for all Black men held in federal, state, county and city prisons and jails.
>
> We want all Black people when brought to trial to be tried in court by a jury of their peer group or people from their Black Communities...
>
> We want land, bread, housing, education, clothing, justice and peace...[59]

The Black Panthers initially expressed little interest in whites; instead, they determined to seek justice on their own "by any means necessary."[60] This approach was a far cry from the inclusive appeal of civil rights leader Rev. Martin Luther King Jr. But King was dead, assas-sinated in 1968. That year the Black Panthers enlarged the scope of their activities from self-protection and free breakfast programs for children to identifying as a "revolutionary internationalist" group, emphasizing a Marxist-Leninist class analysis of society.[61]

The Panthers cut startlingly dramatic figures in public—glaring, gun-toting blacks with afros, and sporting black berets and black leather jackets. They talked of violent revolution with phrases like "pick up the gun" and "off the pig." White radicals in the New Left began to lionize the Panthers, and this fascination increased after Party cofounder Huey Newton, imprisoned on charges that he gunned down an Oakland police officer, claimed he'd been falsely accused.[62] Soon a "Free Huey" campaign formed to support him. At its center was a ubiquitous photograph of the handsome young man sitting enthroned, with spear and rifle, on a wicker chair. Shouts of "Free Huey!" were taken up by college demonstrators across the land.

Such talk alarmed the white power structure, which responded with deadly force. FBI chief J. Edgar Hoover was especially eager to neutralize the Black Panthers. As a result, Panthers were spied on, arrested, and at least 24 were killed or wounded in shootouts with police between 1967 and 1969.

In June 1970 the Black Panthers called for a constitutional convention. The beneficiaries of the new document would be not only black people, but also other ethnic minorities, youth, women, young men fighting wars, and the elderly.[63] All well and good, although nobody mentioned gays.

Then, in a speech on Aug. 15, 1970,[64] Huey Newton—just days out of prison[65]—called for Black Panther acceptance of women's liberation and gay liberation. In prison, Newton had apparently been thinking through how he felt about women and gays, and he shared his own insecurities: "Sometimes our first instinct is to want to hit a homosexual in the mouth and to want a woman to be quiet." Why? We want to hit a homosexual "because we're afraid we might be homosexual," and shut a woman up "because she might castrate us." But, he reasoned, "we must gain security in ourselves and therefore have respect and feelings for all oppressed people."

But he went further than mere acceptance: " ...Maybe I'm now injecting some of my prejudice by saying, '*Even* a homosexual can be a revolutionary. Quite the contrary, maybe a homosexual could be the *most* revolutionary." He advised his followers to be "careful about using terms which might turn our friends off...'faggot' and 'punk' should be deleted from our vocabulary."[66]

This surprise welcome thrilled GLFers across the country. Many gay radicals felt that they were merely tolerated by others in the New Left, that their issues—homophobia, heterosexual oppression—were considered less important than, say, ending the war in Vietnam. Newton's statement signaled not only a link with the struggle against racism, it meant validation within the larger movement. Suddenly, with this blessing, gays now seemed to be in the vanguard of the revolution, alongside the Panthers.

A plenary session for the convention was held at Temple University in Philadelphia in early September.[67] The many sessions included workshops on liberation struggles around the world.[68] Even a workshop on self-determination for high school students took place, and its participants proclaimed, "Long live Marxism-Leninism-Mao-Tse-Tung thought!!!!"[69]

Not surprisingly, people with widely different backgrounds and priorities clashed at the Philadelphia session. Lesbian feminist Lois Hart approached the session with elation. As she later wrote, consciousness of heterosexual oppression of women and gays would finally link with the struggle against racism to create "a public revolutionary document, perhaps the first manifesto of the New World, its consciousness complete." Then, in a meeting with the "super butch" Panthers, she began to question the need for a new constitution. The response, as she wrote, was immediate: "The room exploded and hummed with long harangues by black women and men who were outraged at my white thin-skinnedness, my racism, my gross lack of empathy and awareness of Black oppression." Other gay people later told her that she seemed to be talking down to the Panthers. "I began to understand a little," she wrote. "Two groups, one Black, one Gay—both locked inside our awarenesses of all the gross and subtle tones and manners designed to keep us down."[70]

But when it became clear that gay women were expected to "bear revolutionary babies"[71] instead of having autonomomy, the gay women's caucus walked out of the RPCC plenary session.[72]

About 100 gay men attended the Philadelphia gathering.[73] A few of them dressed in drag for rap sessions with the Panthers.[74] For one delegation, the event was inspirational: The Panthers "treated us with respect and consideration; not acting judgmentally toward what was unfamiliar or even strange to them." As a result, the delegates "acted in a new way toward each other. We weren't sex-subjects or sex-objects; we were people who were beginning to love each other. We touched each other a lot, not because of someone being 'cute' or 'groovy' but to give warmth and support ... We also listened to each other more, with more respect ..."[75] In compiling a list of demands to be read before the entire session, the need for Third World leadership in gay liberation became increasingly clear: "We realized that we couldn't progress as a group unless we fought racism in ourselves and in the society we want to change...."[76]

And since blacks and Chicanos wore distinctive berets, the gay men devised their own berets made of multicolored yarn. When the gay liberationists marched into an assembly of revolutionary peoples, they raised their clenched fists to express solidarity, but with limp wrists, a camp gesture no one else seemed to understand.[77]

The women's walkout in Philadelphia created a sense that the session was incomplete.[78] But other groups, through discussion and "struggle," assembled lists of demands and recommendations for the new constitution. So, on to Washington to create the new document out of the various radical groups' demands. In D.C., preparations had been underway to host the event. The Black Panthers needed food, housing and monetary donations. In response, the GLF commune on S Street threw a fundraising party and invited other gay liberation organizations to stay at the commune for the weekend.[79]

As for real interaction between the newly established D.C. Black Panther chapter and GLF-DC, both groups were apparently preoccupied with their own tasks and issues, and neither group made any effort to meet, recalled GLFer and physician Tim Tomasi, who for a time became the go-to doctor for D.C.'s Black Panthers. He talked up gay liberation with the few Panthers he had contact with, but his impression was that "they thought that gay liberation was relatively low on the list of politically important things."[80]

Still, after months of discussion, gays were feeling a renewed sense of purpose. Huey would appear in person. Big things were expected of him, but he was equal to the challenge. Somehow he would unite the many squabbling caucuses of the movement—Students for a Democratic Society, women's liberation, the Puerto Rican gang the Young Lords, "street people,"[81] Yippies, the "Asian American Front Against Fascism,"[82] gays and lesbians, to name a few—and the radical left would take a big step forward.

Check-in began early Friday morning, Nov. 27, at All Souls Uni-tarian Church on 16th Street NW.[83] The platform workshops would take place on Friday and Saturday, and Saturday evening the attending groups would present their demands to the convention as a whole. Climaxing the event, Newton would speak.

THINGS WENT WRONG immediately. Howard University had agreed to rent the university gymnasium for the convention but, two days beforehand, balked because the Panthers had failed to meet a deadline for payment of a rental fee.[84] The Panthers lashed out, accusing local and federal officials of sabotaging the event. In a press release they called Howard a factory that produced black robots willing to serve "the capi-talist-racist slave master," with special venom directed toward Howard's president, James Cheek, and his "Negroe [sic] flunky administrators."[85] (Cheek had announced, when he took the job leading Howard in 1969, a time of student unrest, that he would not work "under intimidation, vio-lence or coercion of any kind."[86] Still, considering the radical nature of the gathering, Cheek may have been under outside pressure to separate Howard from the convention.)

Other venues around town were already arranged for parts of the convention—including several churches[87]—so some of the meetings could take place as planned. But losing Howard, with its historical and cultural resonance and the space it could provide, was a crippling blow. Having no convention "center" created a sense of disarray among the roughly 4,000 (mostly young and white)[88] people who came to town.

Some 300 representatives of gay liberation groups nationwide had gathered, perhaps the largest such gathering since the movement began the year before.[89] Many gays were staying at American University's Kay Spiritual Life Center. The chapel served as both dormitory and meeting hall for the men. Others were put up at the GLF commune, with delega-tions from Kentucky, Florida, Kansas, Boston and New York squeezed into the household. One visitor there described wall-to-wall men rap-ping, flirting and consciousness-raising, a scene of "gay revolutionary hippie chaos."[90]

But there were casualties. The Boston delegation left town abruptly, leaving a letter to explain that "each one of us has had to endure 48 hours of cruising, of constant pressure to get a piece of ass for the night…The pain of finding yourself on a meat rack when you came to be with brothers is too much to endure…we must go back to Boston and…create people who will never oppress each other the way we have been oppressed here."[91]

But there was little time to ponder Boston's sensitivity. At a daylong gay male workshop held on Friday at American University, Tom Ashe took notes and helped guide the session.[92] The main purpose was to review the gay men's statement drawn up at Philadelphia, but other issues kept cropping up: the lack of women in GLF, the problems of transvestites and transsexuals, femmes feeling oppressed by butches,[93] classism, open relationships. Then there were digressions on self-defense, gays in the military, anarchy, the nuclear family, mental institutions, the church, gay studies, gay genocide, ecology and racism.[94] Despite the multitude of issues, gays had one more day to finalize their demands before presenting them to the convention late Saturday.

A rally on Friday evening attracted several thousand activists to Malcolm X (Meridian Hill) Park on 16th Street.[95] The Panthers had managed to obtain a last-minute permit for the use of the crime-ridden park, and the rally revived spirits deflated by the confusion permeating the convention. The Panther band entertained, and a Panther representative spoke, to shouts of "Free Bobby Seale!/Free Angela [Davis]!/Free Ericka [Huggins]!"[96] When the speaker trashed fascism, racism, capitalism and imperialism, the gays added, "Sexism!"[97] They formed a huge circle[98] and snake-danced in their colorful berets.[99] They also trotted out several chants:

> "Two, four, six, eight, Gay is just as good as straight."[100]
> "Go left, go gay, now pick up the gun."[101]
> "Hey, hey, what do you say, try it once the other way."[102]
> And *(to the tune of "Auld Lang Syne"):*
> "We're here because we're queer."[103]

Which displays of liberation may have been too much for some Panther marshals, who heckled the gays in high-pitched voices.[104] Others in attendance were also displeased. "Damn faggots" was heard when the gays walked among the crowd urging people to affirm their homosexuality and their love for their brothers and sisters. "But despite some ill feeling," one black participant recalled, "we remained gay, beautiful and proud. It was a trip which compared only to the Christopher Street March."[105] In Malcolm X Park, another said, "we left our closets behind. For many of us who had for years felt alienated within the movement… it was a new kind of experience. We sang, we danced, we hugged, we were proud and happy."[106]

A few hours later, early on Saturday, Nov. 28, about 50 proud and unhappy gay men were milling around in the Zephyr. Tom Ashe and the others had driven back to the American University chapel and shared their experience with others staying there. Discussion was heated. Finally several carloads of men—some wearing lipstick or bits of female attire,[107] a couple grabbing signs such as "Gay Is Good"[108]—were on their way to the restaurant. The plan, such as it was, was to protest the denial of service, to see to it that gays were served,[109] to get an apology from the management,[110] but at least to zap the Zephyr: Invade, disrupt, express outrage and leave.[111] As a participant later wrote in the *Chicago Seed*, "The militant atmosphere of the RPCC…had made us aware of our strength, and had infected us with the spirit to march right in to the heart of the monster."[112]

The group arrived at the still-busy bar around 1:30 a.m.[113] Some of the men sat down at the few free tables; others did a little impromptu consciousness-raising by explaining to patrons what had happened[114] and declaring, "Out of the closets and into the streets!"[115] Then things got more provocative. Somebody put a coin in the jukebox, and a couple of men started dancing. Somebody kissed a customer on the forehead. Ramos went up to the manager and said, "I told you we'd be back, honey, and now you're gonna serve us."[116] The manager told everyone in the bar to leave.[117] The gays didn't want to leave before the other patrons. In the confusion, with people moving toward the exit,[118] and with testosterone flowing on both sides, things turned violent.

Whoever made the first move, shoving somehow became punching, then a free-for-all. Beer bottles, salt shakers and mugs went flying. Furniture was overturned. "I managed to throw a beer in one man's face, and an ashtray full of ashes and butts into another's as I was standing on a table," Ashe remembered. "But then I was dragged from the table to the floor and was being punched in the sides until I got up and managed to punch two men backwards and knock them onto the floor."[119] Elsewhere, a gay man ended up hiding under a table. "Two guys were going to beat up on me," he said, "so I asked them if they wanted to have sex instead." That seemed to stop them.[120]

The fighting spilled onto Wisconsin Avenue. The gays scattered, regrouped. Police arrived. Ashe recalled that two men were beating Ramos in the street, and he went to help his boyfriend. Then the manager pointed out Ashe and Ramos as the troublemakers. The police pushed Ramos and Ashe against a car and frisked them.[121] Somehow, in the confusion, the police did not detain the gay men. They all got back to their van, which was parked about a block away. They sent scouts back to the Zephyr to make sure that all the gay men had gotten out. Finally, they pulled away from the curb and onto Wisconsin Avenue. Within seconds the police stopped the van and arrested the 12 men in it.

The final score: The large glass window in the front of the bar was shattered. Two bar employees were taken to the hospital and required stitches, one of them knocked out cold.[122] The "fairies" walked away from the brawl with minor cuts and bruises. With their makeup and outlandish attire, "we looked like easy pickings," said one participant.[123] They weren't.

SATURDAY MORNING a call came in to Georgetown University's E. Barrett Prettyman Program (known as the Georgetown Legal Interns). The two-year graduate program, designed to train trial defense lawyers, had the reputation of representing political protesters. When GLF called, a Legal Interns representative agreed to go to the police lockup. There he found, amid the night's crop of arrestees, an agitated group of 12 men in a large holding cell.[124]

The group was hardly a defense lawyer's ideal. Here was a hodge-podge of the non-employed and the professional. Some sullen, uncommunicative guys had police records, mostly for drug possession. One was an Army veteran. Eight of the men were white, two were black and two Latino.

Among the arrestees were four for whom the ordeal lasted longest: Skinny, funny and flamboyant Washingtonian José Ramos, 18, was a high school graduate. Also from D.C., Terry Leigh, 24, described himself as a freelance artist and student; acquaintances described him as gentle, androgynous, "anarchistic" (at least according to Bruce Pennington). The Chicago con-

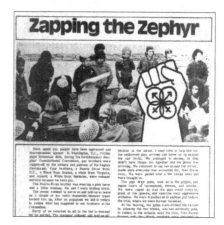

Wearing distinctive berets, the D.C. 12 read a statement about their oppression. (Philadelphia Gay Dealer, ca. December 1970, courtesy Decio Sales-Filho)

tingent included Michael Goldberger, 35, assistant professor of anatomy at the University of Chicago, who as a highly educated man of an older generation, might show up in khakis, a button-down oxford shirt and a string of beads.[125] Tom Ashe, from Oakland, California, was unemployed but had an M.A. in psychology from Temple University. He had attended the Christopher Street celebration in New York earlier in the year and become a passionate gay radical.

Overnight, the police had taken the 12 men[126] to a police substation and put them in a cell. (A GLF newsletter asserted that the police had called them "fags" and "fairies," to which the gays responded with "manifestations of their revolutionary love.")[127] Later in the night, the complaining witnesses from the restaurant went to the substation to file formal complaints. Saturday afternoon at their arraignment, the 12 pleaded not guilty to charges of simple assault, destruction of property, unlawful entry. A jury trial was demanded, and all were released on personal recognizance.

A pro-bono defense team formed quickly, mostly from the Georgetown Legal Interns program and the Legal Aid Agency. The team included John Zwerling and interns Charles W. Daniels, Peter Weisman and Laurence B. Finegold. Two women on the defense team stand out:

Mary-Helen Mautner, 26, is now recalled chiefly through the Mautner Project for Lesbians With Cancer, established after her death in 1989. If Mautner was out as a lesbian in 1970, she was so subtle about it that her fellows on the defense team were not aware of it, including the one defense lawyer likeliest to recognize a kindred spirit, Renee Hanover, who traveled from Chicago to help out.

BORN IN 1926, Hanover came late to law, and left a marriage after she realized she was a lesbian and wanted to live openly as one.[128] Being a single mother and an unapologetic lesbian was not easy:

> I was about to graduate from law school when somebody informed my dean that I was a lesbian. I had to have a hyster-ectomy at the time. So I was thrown out of law school in '65. And my lover committed suicide while I was in the hospital. Times were tough. I may sound like a ball-breaker but believe me…They were going to be sorry about all of this, as far as I was concerned. And I was arrogant enough to say to myself, "Nobody else is going to kill themselves."[129]

She was admitted to the Illinois bar in 1969. She helped form Chicago Gay Liberation Front and did legal work with the Black Panthers and other radical groups, as well as representing conscientious objectors.[130]

One of the Zephyr arrestees from Chicago had suggested contacting her,[131] and she came to Washington and met with the legal team. She later told me she was the only openly gay person on the team.[132] "My reason for even getting in these cases was to publicize things, to show people you can fight back," she said. "There was never any group trial of homosexuals before this." Gays had been criminally charged as individuals but never as a group.[133] So what seemed to other members of the legal team to be an ordinary case of a bar brawl[134] seemed, to Hanover, to be historic.

Most of the men arrested were required to stay in Washington for six weeks to await the hearings and trial. The two white Chicagoans with academic jobs were allowed to return home while black and Puerto

Rican defendants had to remain in Washington until the trial, Ashe noted bitterly in an article he wrote for an underground newspaper.[135] The defendants stuck in Washington needed a place to stay, and the GLF commune agreed to take them in. The residents set up cots in the basement for the men and also provided Renee Hanover accommodations.

With a defense team in place, the gay revolution now had to face justice. The team began working up a defense with the "D.C. 12"—as the men dubbed themselves à la the Chicago Seven in the radical-cause style of the time.

But communication could be difficult. One member of the legal team said he was now forced to process the concept of gay "rights" he learned about in law school; he found there was a difference between comfortable intellectualizing and dealing with his own visceral reactions.[136] One of the defendants felt the defense team didn't understand them. "They tried to be nice to us because we were supposedly leftists," he said, but "we were queers."[137] Some of the gays didn't help matters by engaging in outlandish behavior. Leigh and Ramos tended to start camping, and Leigh once even took off his boots and "snorted" them in front of lawyers, just to get a reaction.[138] Even for Hanover, whom some saw as a kind of den mother, it could be hard getting a few of the men to settle down. She had to tell them, "We're on a different kind of mission here. Cut the nonsense."[139]

The filing of pretrial motions began on Jan. 15, 1971. Pretrial motions are attempts by both sides in a case to determine whether the case should be dismissed or, if not, what evidence and witnesses can be presented. Such motions set boundaries for the trial and determine what legal arguments may be made. Most pretrial motions consist of opposing attorneys arguing before a judge, but sometimes a kind of "mini-trial" can take place in which witnesses can be presented. There is no jury for these arguments; the judge makes the decisions about the evidence going forward. That is what happened with the D.C. 12.

The first argument the defense made toward suppressing evidence was that the arresting officers did not have probable cause to arrest each of the 12 defendants. That reasoning gained no foothold with Dyer Justice Taylor, an experienced Federal Power Commission officer hearing his first criminal case.[140]

The second defense argument was based on what the 12 men claimed happened on the night of the arrest. They said the police brought the bar witnesses into the substation lockup to identify them as the perpetrators, even opening the cell door so they could get a better look at the men. The police allegedly conducted what is called a "show-up," according to one Legal Intern. "That's where you just present the suspect to the witness and say, 'Is this the man?' ...that's a surefire way to get an identification of the person shown to you, whether or not they were involved. It's considered impermissibly suggestive generally in the law. ...Once you've made that identification, you always will identify the same person you've identified previously."[141] To avoid the possibility of police directing witnesses to identify innocent persons, victims ordinarily may view suspects only in formal lineups.[142] Defense filed a motion to suppress evidence, based on the alleged show-up, and the judge agreed to hear evidence about this prior to trial.

Meanwhile, a lineup was ordered and took place Jan. 26. In order to make it harder for witnesses to identify people they may already have seen, the defense team began a search to find a "double" for each of the defendants, someone to stand next to each man in the lineup.[143] Word went out not only to the tiny radical gay community but also to friends, students and even a few off-duty police officers. (I got an urgent phone call from the GLF commune to get down to the courthouse and present myself as a possible D.C. 12 look-alike. I did but was not chosen.) The defense managed to assemble up to four look-alikes for each of the 12.[144] The ploy succeeded. After the lineup, the prosecution dropped charges against all but Terry Leigh, José Ramos, Michael Goldberger and Tom Ashe. The D.C. 12 were now four.

On Monday, Feb. 1, Judge Taylor began hearing the arguments for and against suppression of evidence based on the alleged show-up. "We called three or four of our clients to the stand," one defense team member recalled. "They told the story about being arrested in the van, locked up, and the police bringing these people through there in the basement."[145] To avoid a parade of defense witnesses telling the same tale, the judge turned to the other side. So the U.S. attorney started calling her witnesses. As the defense attorney recalled, "She called two or three cops who testified they were there, it didn't happen, it couldn't happen, it wouldn't happen, I had the only keys, nobody went down."[146]

The back-and-forth continued for two weeks. Presented with contrasting scenarios pitting the gays against the police and restaurant employees, Judge Taylor was determined to find who was committing perjury in his courtroom. But even if allowing witnesses to see defendants was improper, what was the remedy? "Is it: well, they shouldn't have done that, but too bad?" one lawyer said. "Or, I think it's so bad that I'm not going to let anybody identify them?"[147] Judge Taylor would have to decide.

THE LEGAL PROCESS soon took on a giddy life of its own. The radical gay community turned out in support and tried to make political theater out of the courtroom proceedings. Defendants and supporters appeared in drag. When one of the defendants was asked to describe the bouncer at the bar, he smiled and said, "Well, judge, he had a nice body."[148] "The courtroom won't be the same," declared a GLF press release. "...Brothers in drag flamed for the court. Defendants came in make-up, jewelry, and much lavender, with words like 'queer,' 'faggot,' and 'cocksucker' coming from the witness stand. We are their worst fears made flesh; we are the vanguard of their liberation."[149]

As the hearing dragged on, witnesses for the two sides tolerated each other's existence in the room they shared. But one day, according to one Legal Intern, the crocheted cap of one defendant, left behind on a chair, disappeared. "It had removed itself from the chair, it had moved itself out the window, and it could be seen in a tree below the window," he said. "We had a half-day hearing while the judge inquired of each and every government witness, who all said they had no idea how that cap traveled from the chair to the tree. After that, they started keeping them in separate witness rooms."[150]

Despite the theatrics, Tom Ashe was worried. As he later wrote:

> When charges were dropped against eight of us, the remaining four felt more vulnerable. We were easier targets for the twenty-eight witnesses who testified against us during the three weeks of preliminary motions. ...The D.C. gay community was always in the courtroom supporting us, and gay

groups in other cities sent what money they could. But when you're on trial and facing sentencing to a D.C. jail you feel alone despite whatever support you get.[151]

Before a jury is selected, the voir dire examination allows attorneys from both sides to question prospective jury panel members to determine if any of them have any knowledge or biases or beliefs that would prevent them from serving impartially. While the daily back-and-forth over the show-up continued, Renee Hanover pursued an idea with potential for future cases involving gay defendants. On February 5, defense attorneys submitted a formal request for the voir dire examination. For the first time, such questions would examine prospective jurors' possible bias against homosexuals, and this request soon became the second main focus of the expected trial.

Hanover worked on an audacious range of issues with the defense team, including: whether such a voir dire was so sensitive that it must be conducted individually, and whether it should be conducted, not by the court but by the defense "because of the insensitivity and lack of knowledge of the court."[152] The reasoning, in part, went something like this: The fight at the Zephyr "was a direct and proximate result of the defendants being not only homosexual; but openly homosexual. That is to say, homosexuality is a way of life to the defendants involved herein."[153] What happened at the Zephyr "was a reaction to a legitimate protest for civil rights. And if people wouldn't recognize that gays had civil rights, then they shouldn't be on the jury. And if they didn't believe that people who had legitimate gripes should be able to protest the denial of those rights, they shouldn't be on the jury."[154] Hanover researched support for the idea of social bias against homosexuals, including a 1963 case in which homosexuals were described as "members of a subhuman, decadent and anti-social culture." The defense concluded by stating that the right to a fair and impartial jury might be denied if the voir dire requests were denied.[155]

No way, said the government lawyers. Having such a voir dire was unnecessary and irrelevant—there were no charges of a sexual nature—and questions about the subject would be inflammatory. The case was about assault, and no one on the jury need know that the defendants were homosexual. Initially, the judge agreed with that argument.[156]

But Hanover kept offering more arguments and data: In Washington, for example, homosexuals were excluded from government employment and were considered security risks; they could be fired from the armed forces, civil service and Department of Defense. So, with a jury made up of 50 percent U.S. government employees being asked to sit in judgment of homosexuals, "the issue is not whether there is anti-homosexual bias, but rather to what degree that bias is present."[157]

Hanover played well to her audience. She reached for the judge's emotions as well as his reason. As a young man during World War II, Dyer Taylor had sustained burns across most of his body in a plane crash. Somehow he'd survived, and he spent two years convalescing in a hospital before undergoing skin grafts to repair his face.[158] Even after plastic surgery, it was obvious he had been in a fire.[159] Hanover suggested that, being different, he understood the oppression gays felt.[160]

Within a week, the court came around to Hanover's requests. Anti-homosexual bias was relevant. Prospective jurors could be questioned individually. The defense could do the questioning. This decision, Hanover later wrote, "is a precedent and an implicit acknowledgment of the sexism of the Amerikan Court System, which has always prevented fair trials for women and homosexuals."[161] She began developing a series of about 100 voir dire questions for prospective jurors.[162]

TOM AND RENEE were both staying at the overcrowded GLF commune. Tom took well to life there. The old townhouse at 1620 S St. NW was the hub of GLF activity in the city, and he found the arrangement chaotic but fun.[163] With the basement setup all mattresses and cots, "it was noisy at night because people would come by stoned at 2 in the morning out of a bar or wherever...So we didn't get much sleep there."[164] But the commune also meant an instant social life. There was always dope around, or cheap jug wine. Even without money, he later recalled, "there was food there, and records. In those days that's really all you needed to keep you going, a few books here and there. I had no possessions."[165]

Amid the fun, another house member recalled that Ashe was so serious and committed to his beliefs that he once became enraged when a visitor used a racial epithet in his presence. "One night we were sitting in my room smoking dope," Bruce Pennington recalled. "And there was this guy there who was very preppy...wearing a trench coat...somebody complimented him on it, and he said, 'Oh, this, I got this at a nigger store downtown.' And Tom Ashe went ballistic. Violently ballistic. And chased the guy downstairs, screaming at him."

For Renee, however, commune life "was just too tumultuous, noisy." She finally asked her associates to find her a different place to stay. As she recalled,

> They finally gave me the address of a lesbian. ...I went there one Friday afternoon, and the woman wasn't home from work yet. So I walked down the block, and there was a restaurant-bar, and I went in. ...I sat there and ordered something, and the man said he didn't have it. And I ordered another thing, and the man said he didn't have it. And I really got mad at him ...So I said, "What is that fellow over there eating?" He said, "A hamburger." I said, "I'll have one too." ...He brought the hamburger and said to me, "Look, don't be upset by anything these guys do in here, because it's payday, and they get excited after working a whole week." I was very angry with him, and I don't think I even responded. The funny thing was...this was a gay bar. And he was worried about me being in the middle of it, either how I felt or how they felt about me.[166]

Hanover shrugged the incident off, yet it may have been another example of gay bars discriminating against their own.

THREE WEEKS INTO the proceedings, on Feb. 17, the legal teams were still treading water about the police show-up. Things were not looking good for the defense. It had the burden of proving that the impropriety had taken place and was faced with the presumption that the police were telling the truth.[167]

After lunch, though, the lead prosecutor requested a recess and the next day announced that the government was dropping the charges: "We have received information which leads us to question the correctness of certain testimony." She declined to elaborate, saying the U.S. attorney's office is "investigating for possible action."[168]

What had happened in the interim was worthy of a TV courtroom drama. A waitress at the Zephyr who had been in the witness room waiting to testify went up to the prosecutor and said, "I can't take this anymore. I've got to get this off my chest." She said that everybody was lying. Of course, witnesses from the bar had been brought down to the lockup. She was there. "The police told us to testify this way," she said. "They said that we had to do that and stick with their story, but it's a lie." She'd been sitting in the witness room listening to everybody laughing about how they were getting away with this story, according to Legal Intern Charles Daniels.

The government's case had collapsed. It was over without ever going to trial.

Judge Taylor, looking sterner than ever, now asked for the police witnesses to be brought into the courtroom. They were lined up against the window and given a lecture on perjury. Taylor told the U.S. attorney to expect indictments. That didn't happen.[169] In a news conference the freed men announced that they would file civil suits for damages resulting from lost jobs, forced travel and uncompensated living expenses during the three-month detention. That never happened.

EVERYTHING HAD COME apart at the Revolutionary People's Constitutional Convention. Back in November, it ended as it began, a shambles. "All we did was stand around waiting for press conferences, announcements, speakers," one woman said. "We couldn't organize our own workshops because people, unbelievably, were made to wait for hours for some usually inconsequential statement."[170]

Interactions with the preoccupied Panthers were cursory. All day Saturday, with no place to go, thousands of participants dawdled along 16th Street between Harvard and Newton streets, where sellers of buttons, underground newspapers and sweatshirts cropped up.[171] The Panthers seemed to want to take charge and assumed the tasks of directing traffic, keeping people on the sidewalks, and keeping "unauthorized" cameramen from taking pictures.[172] One reporter from American University's *Eagle* said that "there were numerous instances when film was destroyed and photographers were threatened."[173] A sense of paranoia reigned, in part because of concern about possible government informers. As for the press, the *Eagle* reported, "The general rule of thumb seemed to be that people did not talk to anyone outside of their particular revolutionary faction. Many participants simply said, 'I don't talk to anyone I don't know.' "[174]

Despite the disruption of the Zephyr arrests, other gay delegates met on Saturday to compile a final list of demands to present to the convention that night. They started with a list made by gay delegates to the Philadelphia plenary session. Again the group Third World Gay Revolution assumed moral authority at the meeting and proceeded to push its own 16-point platform, which the group finally approved.[175] The Third World gay demands mixed elements from the Philadelphia list and the older Panther 10-point program to create a document that appended "Socialism is the answer" to virtually every demand and guaranteed free food, housing, clothing, transportation, etc. for everyone in their new society.[176] I choose to focus instead on the earlier, more general Philadelphia demands. Free of any specific political theory, they seem utopian for the time, more pie-in-the-sky brainstorming than achievable goals. Certainly, most of these demands were not like the laundry list of issues that flew about the room when the delegates met on Friday. Among them:

> The right to be gay anytime, anyplace.
>
> The right to free modification of sex upon demand.
>
> That all modes of human sexual self-expression deserve protection of the law.
>
> Every child's right to develop in a nonsexist, non-possessive atmosphere.
>
> That an educational system present the entire range of human sexuality, without advocating any one form or style.
>
> That language be modified so that no gender takes priority.
>
> That organized religions be condemned for aiding in the genocide of gay people.

That psychiatry and psychology be enjoined from advo-
cating a preference for any form of sexuality.

The abolition of the nuclear family.

The full participation of gays in the people's revolutionary
army.

No revolution without us! An army of lovers cannot
lose![177]

The gays chose representatives to present their demands that night
at a 16th Street church. But when they got there, no delegations were
allowed in.[178] Inside, in what was supposed to be the high point of the
weekend, Huey Newton stood beneath the crucifix and addressed a capacity audience of 600 inside, plus about 2,000 gathered on the sidewalk
outside.[179] He talked of the need to abolish national boundaries in favor
of a socialist world government and about his theory of "intercommu-
nalism." "We must take the wealth and the industrial and technological
base away from the rulers and give them to the people," he said. This
move would lead to the creation of a new intercommunal culture and new
institutions, "but we must first seize power by any means necessary."[180]

About the new constitution, he simply said, "A document does not
give us power...we will hold our Revolutionary People's Constitutional
Convention for a rain check until such a time as we liberate Washington,
D.C., and then we'll hold it in the White House, but we'll call it the
Black House."[181] (Newton was later criticized for using "black house"
and not "people's house," since yellow, red and brown people were also
oppressed.)[182] Despite the shouts of "Right on," Newton's effort seemed
underwhelming.

As people left town, the righteous anger that radicals had brought
to the convention now turned to irritation, and revolutionary criticism
devolved into plain old blame. There was plenty to go around. Blame
Howard University for refusing to bend a bit about renting facilities,
blame the Panthers for exercising "almost fascist control and security,"
blame white groups for collapsing in their efforts to provide necessary
services.[183] At Howard, where students felt no particular allegiance to
Newton or the Marxist ideology of the Panthers,[184] the student newspaper blamed the Panthers for failing to negotiate the use of facilities and

News clips, from left: Come Out! Washington Post, Washington Daily News.

for associating with "white fags and rejects."[185] Infatuated white radicals who had looked to the Black Panther Party to promote a strong sense of black-white revolutionary unity now left Washington "depressed, frustrated and complaining," wrote the *Quicksilver Times.* "The power of the people didn't mesh somehow," one white radical complained. "Nothing was accomplished."[186]

The Black Panther Party was slowly weakened by internal conflicts and the external efforts of the FBI. Huey Newton had trouble with the law for the rest of his life and died on the streets of Oakland, California, in 1989.[187] The radical Gay Liberation Front in Washington began to fade and was largely replaced by the well-organized Gay Activists Alliance of Washington later in 1971. Renee Hanover wrote a journal article on the voir dire questions she developed, but since the government dropped the case, her precedent was never formally recognized.[188] Her law career was marked by a number of cases involving gender, LGBTQ issues and race, and she was inducted into the Chicago Gay and Lesbian Hall of Fame in 1991. Tom Ashe eventually became Director of Marketing for Latin America at Digital Equipment Corporation.

The 10-point program created by the Panthers in 1966—and in particular its five demands for "full employment," "decent housing," "education that teaches us our true history," an end to police brutality, and the release of all incarcerated black men—seems much less revolutionary today than it did in the '60s. And largely unrealized still.

As of 2018, African Americans had made some gains but fell behind whites in other areas. High school and college graduation rates among blacks increased dramatically over 50 years, but blacks were only half as likely as whites to have a college degree.[189] Black history is taught in schools, but some teachers barely move beyond mentions of slavery and the civil rights period.[190] In 2018, black workers earned less than whites; blacks were more than twice as likely as whites to live in poverty; and the black unemployment rate was about twice that of whites. Black homeownership in 2015 was just over 40 percent, "a figure virtually unchanged since 1968."[191] Police brutality has persisted, giving rise to the Black Lives Matter movement and the nationwide demonstrations after the death of George Floyd under the knee of a white police officer in 2020. As to freedom for those incarcerated, the rate of blacks in prison or jail nearly tripled between 1968 and 2016 and in 2018 was "more than six times the white incarceration rate."[192]

The demands of gays at the RPCC, on the other hand, have in part been fulfilled. Sodomy is legal nationwide. Nonsexist education and nonsexist language have been widely adopted. Many organized religions have come to welcome gays. Psychiatry abandoned its categorization of homosexuality as an illness. Gays, lesbians and bisexuals may serve openly in the military. (Not part of the wish list: same-sex marriage is legal, and the adoption of children by same-sex married couples is legal.) And these gains were accomplished with relatively little bloodshed.

The new U.S. Constitution was never completed.

BUT FOR ME IT'S STILL
SO SLOW - UNSPONTANEOUS.
LABORED PICTURES OF
IMAGES OF THE VISION
SURE THERE ARE TIMES
WHEN IT'S REAL
THIS LIBERATION
SOMETIMES WHEN MAKING
LOVE OR WORKING TOGETHER
ON THE NEWSPAPER OR
HEARING THAT SOMEONE
YOU KNOW HAS COME OUT.

BUT DISTANT FROM ME
NOW LYING HERE ON A RAINY
DAY IN A STRANGE CITY
TRYING TO CREATE
SOMETHING OUT OF THIS
RECENT CELIBACY

Motive, *1972*

Motive (Lesbian/Feminist Issue), *1972 (pen and ink by B. Vogel)*

War, American style, is a man's game, where to prove his masculinity,
he must maim or kill women, children, the very old, the very young,
and his own brothers. War is an extension of our own oppression because it reinforces the masculine image of males and forces them into
playing roles where the end result is the death of millions of people.

We as gays are a part of the struggle of the Vietnamese, Laotian, and
Cambodian people and feel solidarity with them. In this spirit we sign
this treaty of peace, love and struggle.

*May Day flyer courtesy Tom Ashe; news
clip* Washington Post

*Frank Kameny ran as an openly gay
candidate for a congressional position
in 1971. (Rainbow History Project)*

CHAPTER 6

GLF Sings Backup

IN JANUARY 1971, while GLFers were busy protesting bar discrimination and supporting the D.C. 12 awaiting trial, homophile leader Frank Kameny was quietly in the ascendant. A quirk of history presented him with a unique opportunity to run for a political office of national importance. Over the next six months, GLF divided its attention among helping out with his campaign, participating in an assault on the psychiatric establishment, and taking part in a huge May 1971 antiwar protest. But in the shifting political winds, the gay radicals were going from one action to another, usually as supporting players, and by summer the end of the organization was imminent.

The residents of the District of Columbia—essentially voteless since 1875—suddenly had the opportunity to elect a nonvoting delegate to the U.S. House of Representatives in January 1971. The District government had been run for nearly a century by a congressional committee and a commission appointed by the president. Washingtonians couldn't even vote for a presidential candidate until 1964. But now, with a special election quickly set for March 23, time was tight for selecting a delegate. Some obvious names—including Mayor-Commissioner Walter Washington and civil rights activist Walter Fauntroy—were considered likely candidates for the position.

Then Frank Kameny entered the race. Friends had encouraged him to make this bold move, and after considering the historic nature of such a bid, he decided to go for it. Despite the hard work involved in a campaign, the Mattachine Society veteran would be the star of his show—with advisers, managers and worker bees to help out. Since a victory seemed far from likely for an oddball candidate, one of the main selling points for entering the race was the media coverage each candidate would receive. All the candidates would be given equal time at any radio or TV appearance, including 90-minute TV debates. So Kameny would have a chance to let Washington know that Gay Is Good.[1]

Kameny announced his candidacy at a Feb. 3 news conference[2] and instantly settled nicely into political theater mode. Asked by reporters how he thought he would get along with fellow congressmen if elected, Kameny drolly replied, "I thought there would be no trouble, since we assumed that the same 10% of Congress as of all other groups were homosexual, and that therefore there were some 40 to 50 gay congressmen."[3] He ran as an independent, on a "personal freedom" platform, and threw himself into campaigning. He was always mentioning gay rights, of course, particularly employment discrimination, but he also discussed crime, drug addiction and other issues of general interest to D.C. residents.[4] Polled on topics of interest to the city's gay population, such as sodomy laws and security clearances, all the other candidates expressed some degree of support, although Fauntroy said he "would not like to see further proselytizing," and Democrat Eldridge Parks, an insurance executive, said he "wouldn't want to see a guy show up at the office in a dress."[5]

When longtime Kameny associate Paul Kuntzler went to a GLF meeting to solicit volunteers for the campaign, "the place was jampacked with young gay men," he recalled. They were "energetically involved in a discussion of ageism, sexism and racism." He enlisted several people. One GLFer wrote a campaign speech for Kameny, which the candidate reluctantly decided to give "because he didn't like to do anything that wasn't his idea," Kuntzler said.[6]

The immediate challenge was getting Kameny's name on the ballot, which required 5,000 registered voters to sign a petition supporting his candidacy by Feb. 22.[7] Kameny's advisers estimated they would need about 6,000 signatures just to offset any signatures that might be challenged and thrown out. With less than three weeks to go, GLF and Mattachine Society volunteers worked gay bars, shopping areas and other locations,[8] but progress was slow. Then someone came up with a saving idea: Ask the Gay Activists Alliance in New York to send volunteers to D.C. to help collect signatures. Bus transportation and local hosts were quickly arranged,[9] and by the end of the voter drive, with the help of the GAA volunteers, the Kameny campaign had more than enough signatures.[10]

On March 23, voting day, it was Democrat Walter Fauntroy, a protégé of Martin Luther King, who won.[11] (His successor, Eleanor

Holmes Norton, began serving in Congress in 1990.)[12] Kameny took a mere 1,841 votes.[13] But the campaign was a learning experience for Kameny and his followers, and it established the "gay vote" more firmly in the local political arena. And, as one campaign volunteer recalled, it was "real."[14]

After the election, inspired by the participation of New York GAA, a D.C. Gay Activists Alliance formed.[15] GAA (now called GLAA) used such tools as candidate questionnaires and confrontations with public officials to achieve civil rights for gays. For a time, the "membership" of both GLF and GAA was fluid, with people participating in activities related to both.

Meanwhile, at the end of February 1971, GLF meetings moved from Grace Episcopal Church in Georgetown to St. James Episcopal Church in Capitol Hill,[16] "in order to be closer to the black community," as *D.C. Gazette* freelancer Tom Shales wrote. But the decision to relocate didn't solve anything. "If the move has made the meetings more convenient for some…it has made them much less accessible to others."[17] The gay communes in Dupont Circle were within walking distance of Georgetown, whereas Capitol Hill was much harder to get to. And mere geographical proximity to African American gays in the eastern half of the city did not guarantee that they would come to meetings. Attendance dropped off.

NO SOONER WAS THE SPECIAL election over than a nationally organized May Day antiwar rally was approaching. The concept for this unprecented gathering of New Left "tribes" was simple: "The government has not stopped the Vietnam War, so we will stop the government."[18] Planned nonviolent actions, scheduled around May 1, the traditional International Workers' Day, would take place all over the Washington area, especially a major disruption of Monday morning rush-hour traffic, all in an attempt to shut the federal government down for a day.

Since many GLFers were active in the antiwar movement, it was a given that GLF would stake out territory in this event. But radical gays were feeling, at best, halfheartedly welcomed into May Day decision-making.[19] In New Left planning meetings in early 1971, straight white men seemed to be telling everyone else what to do and shoving the concerns of gays aside: Stop the war first, then deal with a range of lesser issues and isms.[20] This struck gay activists as homophobic. As activist and filmmaker John Scagliotti recalled, planning meetings would begin in an orderly fashion with an agenda:

> [But] the agenda never talks about the major identity things that we wanted to talk about: gay people, women, or other stuff. So at some point in any given meeting, a gay person would get to the microphone and say (what I call "the moment"): "You people are a bunch of racists," or "You people are a bunch of sexists or a bunch of homophobes." At that moment people in the crowd would scream and yell: "C'mon! We had an agenda. We had an agreement. This is stuff that can be talked about later"...there was never a point where you could talk about these things. So there was always tension.[21]

Radical gays decided to largely separate themselves from the May Day organization and plan their own actions as Gay May Day. In Washington, a Gay May Day Tribe office was set up to organize actions, housing and publicity,[22] and then to coordinate with the umbrella May Day organizers.[23]

By Saturday, May 1, some 35,000 protesters had already set up camp in a festival atmosphere in West Potomac Park near the Washington Monument—or Algonquin Peace City, as organizers dubbed it.[24] They pitched tents, enjoyed free food, heard speakers, discussed the coming actions, and listened to a rock concert.[25] New York activist Perry Brass arrived in West Potomac Park on Saturday and made his way to the tents where gay liberation flags were flying. He met people from as far away as Alaska, some of whom had been there for several days. Many people were in some degree of drag, or wore nothing. That afternoon, rally speakers included women demanding that men confront their own sexism and stop harassing women at the event, which speech was met with some derision. The rock concert continued into the evening.[26]

That night, Scagliotti, feeling full of the romance of revolution, walked through the campground and saw the entire area lit with bonfires. "It looked as if the radicals had taken over the city," he recalled.

I felt like a lieutenant in this military action that was ready to take place...I'm walking through the campsite feeling like a big shot. I was about 20, a kid and a hippie. I would encourage people: affinity groups I had gotten to know over the phone ... Then at this one campsite there was this gorgeous man sitting by himself...I went and talked with him. We ended up in a tent ...After a while I hear these funny noises and screaming and yelling. I look out, and there on the other side a good, good distance I could see there were eight bulldozers. Nixon had sent in bulldozers that night just to clean the place out at 12 o'clock. The bulldozers were coming, and people were running. Tents are being squashed. And I was having sex.

Scagliotti had a climactic decision to make. "...I remember calculating how much time I had until the bulldozers would get to our tent... So I went back [inside the tent] thinking, 'Gee there's about three or four minutes. I can do it.' And by then the crowd had rushed so much that the tent was crashing down from people running into it. I never saw this guy again."[27] Algonquin Peace City was history. The camping permit had been abruptly withdrawn, and officers were busting the place up.[28] Many protesters left the city at this low point.

But others in the Gay May Day Tribe, apparently anticipating trouble, had already packed up and moved to Georgetown. They ended up at Grace Church, the original site of GLF meetings, where they had permission to spend Sunday night. In preparation for the Monday morning traffic shutdown, the protesters discussed tactics for dealing with the police. Some old hands shared war stories of other protest marches while medical volunteers prepared bandages nearby. Then the reality of what he was about to encounter settled on Brass. "All I felt was really queazy [sic] anxiety and looking at my sisters and brothers and feeling how could anyone want to hurt them, they were so beautiful?" he recalled. "I asked one of my brothers who had been in Viet Nam what it was like 'waiting' and he said it was the way we felt that night...things were looking quite 'heavy.' "[29]

The group at Grace Church got up around 4:30 a.m. on Monday to rumors of police making mass arrests everywhere.[30] In fact, some 10,000 troops were assigned to various locations around Washington—including monuments, parks and traffic circles. The number ranged from federal troops to National Guardsmen to the D.C. Metropolitan Police, with 4,000 more held in reserve.[31]

The band of radical men and women paused to link arms and "pray for a peaceful day of civil disobedience," then left the church in groups of four and five to get to target areas under cover of darkness. Brass's group, assigned to a location along the major commuter route Rock Creek Parkway, played cat and mouse with police until they were able to scramble down a ravine and get onto the roadway, where they stopped rush-hour traffic for several minutes before police moved in. The demonstrators escaped back up the ravine. With their assigned section of the parkway now controlled by police, Brass and others headed for Dupont Circle. Along the way, they saw that parked cars had been dragged into the street to block traffic. Police and guardsmen ringed the circle, and the air was hazy with tear gas. Buses and vans stood waiting to transport arrestees to a lockup.[32]

Actions happened all over the city. At Wisconsin Avenue and M Street in Georgetown, while other groups chanted or sang songs when they succeeded in building a barricade, "the gay group all started hugging each other," recalled one participant.[33] Elsewhere in Georgetown, "stalled" cars created backups. At George Washington University, students danced in the street and lifted car hoods so drivers would have to get out and close them. Many drivers seemed supportive of the actions.[34]

Protester Don Button encountered one Washingtonian who was not supportive. Button was part of a group trying to shut down the parkway near 23rd and P streets. "I ran down P Street being chased by the cops, and I ran up to this woman's house, and she was standing outside and said, 'Come here! Come here!'" Thinking he'd found a safe haven, he ran toward her. "...and just as I got there she slammed the door, so I was cornered then, and the cops ran up and arrested me." After that, "we were taken to the local precinct in Foggy Bottom," Button recalled. "There were about 30 of us, and they put about 15 of us in a single cell. People were sitting on the bed, and people were sitting on their laps, and the rest of us were standing." To pass the time and keep their spirits up, "we started singing doo-wop and Motown songs."[35]

Radical gay Deacon Maccubbin spent all day frustrated in his attempt to get arrested. "I spent most of my time between the Capitol and the Washington Monument," he recalled, "blocking traffic on 14th Street, sitting down in traffic, getting yoked by a cop and dragged off to the sidewalk. Then the cop would drag someone else off. They beat us with batons, threw tear gas, and we'd run off and start somewhere else."[36]

More than 7,000 protesters were arrested on Monday morning.[37] Police disregarded the niceties of civil liberties and tossed anyone who looked like a potential troublemaker into police wagons. With so many arrestees to hold, authorities set up an emergency detention center next to RFK Stadium—a "concentration camp," as one detainee described it.[38] By afternoon the police had control of Washington and the protest was over. Charges later were dropped against most of those arrested because police had no evidence against them to present in court. (Later, as a result of a class-action lawsuit brought by the ACLU on behalf of protesters who claimed that their constitutional right to free assembly had been violated, settlements were paid out to many who were arrested.)[39]

In the end, although President Richard Nixon (who was in California during the protests) did not give federal workers the day off, most commuters did eventually get to their jobs.[40] So the government did not shut down. Through a huge law enforcement effort, it rolled on, slightly battered and radically inconvenienced. But protesters, largely satisfied that their huge numbers had shown how serious and widespread antiwar sentiment was, also claimed victory.

THE ANNUAL MEETING OF the American Psychiatric Association happened to be taking place at the Shoreham Hotel in a quiet section of Northwest Washington at the same time as the May Day protests. Frank Kameny, with characteristic focus, turned his attention to the convention, where he knew he could make a splash. He had long wanted to take on the APA because of its official position on homosexuality. The APA's *Diagnostic and Statistical Manual of Mental Disorders* categorized homosexuality as a "sociopathic personality disturbance" involving a pathological fear of the opposite sex caused by traumatic parent-child relationships.[41] Kameny had long denounced that definition as barbaric, especially since it was used as a basis for a range of harsh treatments for "curing" homosexuality, and he seized every opportunity to attack psychiatry. On this occasion, he was in the ballroom as an official participant in the conference, since some APA members had helped arrange a panel discussion, "Lifestyles of the Non-Patient Homosexual."[42] GLF and GAA were ready to jointly zap the 1971 conference, although GLFers were now clearly singing backup to GAA's lead.

The American Psychiatric Association's DSM-II labeled homosexuality a sociopathic condition.

GAA members had carefully planned the takeover of the APA meeting. The plotters got floor plans for the Shoreham to determine the best entrances to use,[43] and many zappers secretly approached the hotel from the rear, through wooded Rock Creek Park. Even "arrest teams," volunteers who could occupy the police while others protested, were set up.[44]

The big May 3 target event in the Regency Ballroom was the "ordination of new psychiatrists…with all the elderly psychiatrists sitting up on the podium wearing their gold medals with the ribbons around their necks," as Kameny recalled.[45] In the midst of the dignified proceedings, at an arranged signal, about 50 protesters—including participants from the Gay May Day Tribe and the Mattachine Society—came whooping and hollering into the ballroom, entering through fire doors, marching in the aisles and gathering near the podium.[46] Some of the gays were in bits of drag, with make-up, glitter, wigs, earrings,[47] war paint or feathers.[48] The reaction in the room gave little evidence of professional restraint. Psychiatrists were yelling, "Faggots! Drag queens!"[49] As Kameny recalled, when the protesters tried to get on the platform, "all the elderly psychiatrists proceeded to beat them over the head with their gold medals." Some were shoving and tackling the protesters.[50]

Several copies of the protesters' talking points were apparently distributed among participants, so that whoever got to the microphone first could speak.[51] But of course Kameny, being close, took command. The moderator "said to me, 'What are you doing?' I said, 'I'm seizing the microphone from you.' And he said, 'Well, tell me your name and I'll introduce you.'" He introduced Kameny, "whereupon I proceeded to denounce them as the enemy incarnate." Then someone pulled the plug on the mike. "Well, I have never needed a microphone to be heard," Kameny recalled, "so I just continued to denounce them while the psychiatrists shook their fists at us and called us Nazis."[52]

Kameny's declaration of war against psychiatry included eight demands, among them: that psychiatrists cease using electric shock therapy to try to convert homosexuals, and that homosexuality be permanently removed from the psychiatric list of diseases. In sum, "We demand the treatment of the oppressing society instead of the attempted treatment of us, the oppressed homosexual."[53]

Most of the demonstrators were able to escape without incident; safely back at the GLF commune, people exultantly sang "When the Gays Go Marching In."[54] For Kameny, the invasion was another feather in his cap, and it had its intended effect. Within two years, the American Psychiatric Association diagnostic manual was revised. The sixth printing of the DSM-II in 1974 stopped categorizing homosexuality as sociopathic. All at once, homosexuality by itself did not imply impaired judgment, stability, reliability or general capabilities.[55] As Kameny put it, the 1971 zap was a significant event in "the APA's restoration of gays to health."[56]

BY SUMMER 1971, IT WAS CLEAR that GLF was winding down. In a year, it had grown from an initial gathering of about 40 people to perhaps 120.[57] But the general weekly meetings in Capitol Hill drew fewer and fewer attendees and were discontinued by the end of June. The GLF commune took up the slack by continuing to hold regular weekly meetings.[58] The older Mattachine Society of Washington was also fading, and it suspended regular meetings in October 1971.[59] That left the highly organized Gay Activists Alliance as the main surviving gay organization.

But just as GLF was sputtering, the Skyline Faggots collective formed to prove that the ideals of gay liberation were far from dead.

The author in Israel, 1971.
(Author photo)

CHAPTER 7

Wanderjahr

I DID VERY LITTLE for the gay cause in 1971. In fact, I did very little in general, and I was becoming increasingly anxious in my jobless existence. I spent half of 1971 moving among cheap living quarters, trying not to spend money, and listlessly looking for work. I decided at one point to make a life of selling flowers on the street—perhaps I imagined myself a modern-day Eliza Doolittle—and I obtained a D.C. vendor's license but never followed through. More and more, I wanted to escape again.

The end of the line came in the spring, when I landed in a dreary rooming house on Park Road at the edge of Mount Pleasant. Sharing a single room with two lesbian friends one floor above an insane woman, I subsisted on peanuts, bananas and chocolate milk, somehow thinking they provided the essential nutrients. My roommates and I became friendly with an attractive young couple who lived in the basement, where the husband maintained a collection of snakes in tanks. We soon found out that he turned gay tricks on the side to make extra money and later discovered that he sometimes roughed up his wife, whereupon the three of us made a naive attempt to rescue her. To add to the generally claustrophobic atmosphere, FBI agents knocked on our door one day to question me about one of my roommates. Feeling paranoid and trapped, I turned to a program that sent young people to Israel to work on kibbutzim. A rural life half a world away seemed the perfect solution to my situation, even though I'm not Jewish.

Amazingly, I had saved enough money from unemployment, scrimping and sponging to afford a five-month period abroad, especially because as a working kibbutz volunteer all my living expenses there would be assumed by the kibbutz. Elsewhere I would stay in youth hostels to conserve funds, and I got around Europe by thumbing rides. I left D.C. in June. The parents of one of my roommates cared for the cat Sadie on their West Virginia farm, where she began to revert to the barn cat she had once been, and she eventually disappeared into the countryside for good.

Israel was a cultural jolt. Tel Aviv especially had a military presence such as I had never encountered. And the Israelis I met seemed suspicious of young people in the counterculture, who were mainly foreign travelers. Drugs were strictly forbidden. Some people even thought my long hair was a wig. Things were not cool.

On Degania Alef kibbutz, volunteer life was strictly regimented, and we had little interaction with the regular kibbutzniks. We rose for work at 4 a.m. My main assignment was to tie the bunches of ripening dates to the palm trees to prevent them from breaking off. At around 8, the volunteers returned to the dining hall for a hearty breakfast of hot cereal, eggs, yogurt, cucumbers, tomatoes,

S 2161

MILLER BRIAN F

LICENSED VENDOR
DISTRICT OF COLUMBIA
EXPIRES OCT. 31, 1971

Looking more like Charles Manson than a flower seller, I made a fruitless attempt to find direction in life. (Author photo)

cheeses, tea. Then back to work until noon, when the workday ended because of the extreme heat.

I couldn't seem to connect with anyone. What was I even doing here? Fortunately, one night after some wholesome folk-dance performance put on for the volunteers' benefit, I met Marsha, a New Yorker, who was having a similar reaction, and we began commiserating. Our bond was sealed when I found out that as a waitress in Manhattan, she had served one of my favorite singers, Lotte Lenya! We were now friends for good, and I began to relax.

Afternoons on the kibbutz were free. In the volunteer barracks, we usually napped or read or lolled in one another's rooms playing cards and studying world maps to decide where we might want to travel next. Or, under cloudless skies, we would swim across the Jordan River to a raft in the freshwater Sea of Galilee.

My overseas adventure lasted through October 1971 and included hitching around Great Britain and Crete, then Italy, Austria, West Germany and the Netherlands. When I flew home from Amsterdam, exhausted but refreshed, I settled back into gay life and with a clearer purpose: a need for income.

*1614 S St. NW, home of the Skyline Faggots collective.
(Photo: Steve Behrens)*

CHAPTER 8

A Fresh Start at the Skyline Faggots Collective

MICHAEL FERRI CAME HOME from work one day in early 1971 to find naked men running up and down the stairs of the GLF commune. "We're free! We're free!," they were shouting. "I'm not," he thought to himself. "I'm working to support you all."[1]

At that moment, the one-big-sloppy-family spirit of the commune vanished for Michael, and the need for a new home began to take shape in his mind, a group home of order and quiet dedication to gay liberation.

During the Revolutionary People's Constitutional Convention in November 1970, nine gay out-of-towners had been arrested after the Zephyr bar brawl, and were restricted to Washington to await trial. The GLF commune at 1620 S St. NW took most of them in. Some got jobs and pitched in for rent, but others just hung out. The legal proceedings dragged into February 1971. For a time, between residents upstairs, detainees sleeping on wall-to-wall cots and mattresses in the basement,[2] and assorted friends coming and going at all hours, more than 20 people were living in the house, Michael recalled. Permanent residents tried to stay abreast of the head count, but as one man remembered, "Frequently someone would come running up to the regular house members and say, 'Does anybody know that man in the basement?' "[3]

Ferri felt the chaos keenly. A soft-spoken man, he had briefly been a Roman Catholic seminarian before getting kicked out for homosexual activity. Then he became engaged to a woman, but during the engagement a male friend of theirs seduced him and then abandoned the couple to the wreckage of their relationship.[4] When his Italian-American father asked about the breakup, Michael said, "Dad, I'm gay." Fortunately for Michael, his father was understanding (though Michael did tell me that his father temporarily stopped the family ritual of kissing him in greeting).[5] Now, the naked men on acid pushed Michael to a decision. Within a day, he moved out of the commune and stayed with a friend to regroup and find a way forward.

That way involved the formation of the Skyline Faggots collective. The men of Skyline worked to develop a Marxist analysis of sexual politics, helped produce a magazine and fought homophobia. Along the way, they also discovered that although "the personal is political," the political can get very personal.

IN EARLY 1971 Michael Ferri, Kent Jarratt, Tim Tomasi, Theodore Kirkland and Jim Lawrence were all members of the same consciousness-raising group. Because they cherished the trust and support they got from one another, the men wanted to continue meeting on a more permanent basis, and they began to talk about living together.

Kent Jarratt, right, with his brother Stephen (Author photo)

With his aureole of frizzy hair and slightly bored mien, Kent Jarratt, 22, looked like the true radical of the group. Indeed, he wanted to make gay liberation a part of all the other radical movements swirling around at that time, from feminism to the Black Panthers, and he hoped that somehow people would come together and effect a radical shift in the government.[6] He had dropped out of Miami University after two years, in part because he started telling people he was gay and was getting harassed as a result. Kent had grown up in a foreign service family, but when his father was posted to Libya, families were not allowed to go along because of the unsettled political situation, so he decided to stay in D.C. He got a copyboy job at Newhouse News Service. His handsome older brother, Stephen, also lived in town, and both brothers were involved with the startup of Gay Liberation Front. Kent wanted a closer relationship with the wonderfully imperious Stephen but at the same time was determined to forge his own identity, mainly through writing. A group house would provide the quiet and support he needed for that effort.

Tim Tomasi was hesitating on the verge of a major life decision. He had completed medical school at Georgetown University in 1967[7] and had a residency at D.C. General Hospital. But he dropped out of medicine in 1970 to devote himself to antiwar activities. A neat, dark-haired man whose voice was just above a whisper, he moved into a straight radical commune and was involved in a relationship with a woman there. He knew, though, that he was attracted to men. Rational and analytic, Tim engaged his lover in long discussions about the issue. She calmly accepted his gayness and even encouraged him to check out gay liberation, if only to alleviate his anxieties. He went to New York for the first Christopher Street celebration in 1970 and then excitedly took part in GLF-DC meetings. Still, he loved his woman friend, and he decided to stay faithful to her. For the time being, he would remain in the antiwar house even while mulling his probably irreversible leap into an actively gay life and joining a gay collective.[8]

Theodore Kirkland (I called him "Ted") at 19 was the youngest member and the only African American in the group. Tall and muscular, Ted had come to D.C. seemingly on a whim: In the summer of 1970 he and three white drag queens traveled from Columbus, Ohio, to experience the big (and largely white) Pier Nine superbar, news of which had reached Ohio.[9] Kirkland decided D.C. was where he wanted to be. His personality was often dramatic. Among quiet men, Ted was given to confident declarations and boisterous laughter, and he seemed at ease camping, snapping and attitudinizing to the amusement of others. But he was also thoughtful. He once gave me a little book of mordantly humorous definitions called *Black Is*, which consisted of a series of illustrated examples such as "Black is getting the same treatment by the police whether you're violent or non-violent."[10] And he later recalled enjoying the emotional intimacy of the consciousness-raising group: It was the first time "that I had cried with other men," he said, "that I had struggled with feelings that I just didn't think happened between men."[11]

Having both a father and a stepfather in the military, Jim Lawrence was used to a peripatetic life, and he described his upbringing as "always poor."[12] Perhaps a need to achieve financial stability was one reason why he devoted so much energy to his job for an information systems firm, his entrée into the field of publications design.[13] Tall, all arms and legs, with coat-hanger shoulders and pretty but worried eyes, Jim was just now tiptoeing into gay life. He had fallen in love with a fellow student at Amer-

Jim Lawrence in 1971.
(Photo: Steve Behrens)

ican University, and they had later moved in together in the Maryland suburbs. Jim was gentle and funny with his uncertain lover, and he was slowly and carefully letting the world know about his private life. He could be bashful and painfully polite, but at the same time he was open to new experiences. He started going to GLF meetings before he could persuade his lover to attend, and he had no qualms about taking part in public GLF actions.

Talk of all of them living together moved into high gear when a friend offered the men the weekend use of a house in the Virginia mountains. The five could be alone to discuss what they wanted in a collective.

Only now they were six. Jim's lover joined the group for the weekend.

Sandy-haired David Duty was a quiet, seemingly laid-back man. He came to D.C. from Huntington, West Virginia, to attend American University. His older brother had left West Virginia after enduring harassment for being gay, and the teenage David was traumatized by the bullying because he had never known how to defend his brother. In college, David found antiwar activities much easier to engage with than his own confusing desires. But there he had his first sexual experience of any kind, with Jim Lawrence. Called to appear for his draft physical, and despite his fears, David checked the questionnaire box for "homosexuality." Later, an officer pulled him out of line and grilled him with questions. You engage in sexual relations with multiple men, right? A confused David described being in a loving relationship with one man. Do you know what drag is? He didn't. Anal intercourse? No. Ultimately, the interviewer classified him 4-F anyway.[14] David was now free to be with his lover.

But he was uneasy about the prospect of being stuck in the mountains with a bunch of gay men he didn't know well. He worried that the weekend was going to involve some kind of orgy. To his relief, much of the time was spent in discussion of what it meant to be gay in a heterosexual male-dominated world. He began to relax.[15]

David Duty (Jim Lawrence photo courtesy David Duty)

Expectations about living together were as varied as the six men. Michael wanted a disciplined space where he could explore the politics of living as a gay man. Jim had a more generalized concept of being a gay activist in "a living situation that would be comfortable for everyone."[16] For David, a space where he could "get in touch with feelings" was exactly what he needed, especially those relating to his conflicted emotions about being in a monogamous relationship.[17] Ted expected "a seven-day-a-week consciousness-raising situation."[18] Tim and Kent wanted to explore Marxism. As Kent said, "Our aims were to have a Marxist perspective on gay rights and to inject gay rights into the radical movements in D.C."[19] Somehow, the men all meshed, agreeing that they wanted a family atmosphere and a commitment to mutual support as they figured out what being radically gay meant. The decision was made. They would be a collective.

The group needed a name. The word "skyline" came up twice that weekend: They were traveling through the Shenandoah on Skyline Drive, and an Elton John song came on the car radio: "Skyline pigeon fly away." So they decided to call themselves the Skyline Faggots collective.[20] "Faggot" was certainly shocking—a demeaning insult for any male. Jim found that word too confrontational.[21] But the majority decided that by boldly appropriating an insult, they would conquer its negative power. So Faggots they were.

The men found a well-maintained old townhouse to rent at 1614 S St. NW. It had five bedrooms and four fireplaces. The location was just three doors away from the GLF commune, so they would be close to the action but not too close. They moved in around June 1971.

BEGINNING THE adventure was the fun part. The men painted the living room lavender, even the ceiling (a bit much, some later admitted).[22] In the dining room they hung a large purple banner proclaiming, "Skyline Faggots."[23] For the front door, they chose radical red paint, which worked beautifully with the gray stone exterior. "And we kept it closed," said Michael. Skyline was not going to be a community center like 1620. Cleaning and bill-paying were organized. Each member was responsible for cooking dinner once a week.[24] For some, the task of coming home from work and preparing a family meal was a challenge, and no one was a gourmet cook, so some dinners tasted more revolutionary than others.[25] Another house rule: No one was allowed to bring anyone into the house who did not know this was a gay collective.[26] There would be no farcical pretending for the benefit of straight visitors.

Weekly meetings were established to discuss household issues, politics, and to work out any interpersonal issues that might arise. The giving and receiving of revolutionary criticism in a loving atmosphere was part of the deal. The men would struggle through any conflicts that might arise, with group decisions reached. They would all grow from the experience.

Problems arose, of course, but nothing unsolvable. Occasionally, sexual attraction would swirl among the young men. But if a proposition was made and rejected, a heart-to-heart talk usually followed, and feelings were worked through. "In ways that counted, we respected and cared for each other," said Tim.[27]

In general, life on S Street was quiet, supportive, routine. Skyline threw the occasional party and sometimes housed people in town for political purposes, but for the most part the men protected what they had established. They often socialized together, taking weekend walks to Georgetown[28] (walking being the primary mode of transportation, since few young radicals owned cars). Less frequently, they went out to bars as a group. David had never been to a gay bar before, and on one such outing he was startled to see a young man from his hometown high school. Almost instinctively, he hid behind a column, afraid the guy would see him and report back to friends and family at home.[29] For the collective's first Christmas, in 1971, Jim and David got a Christmas tree, baked bread and decorated for a holiday open house.[30] On Christmas

Eve, house members opened presents together at midnight, and there was joy in their world.[31]

If general GLF meetings presented a jumble of political opinions, Skyline would narrow the focus. To understand the political theory behind their oppression, Michael, Tim and Kent formed a reading group to study the history of the left, especially Marxism. (The Black Panther Party had already taken up Marxist class analysis as a way to understand their oppression, and others in the New Left aligned with Marxism in varying degrees.) They read texts by Lenin, Marx and Stalin, then discussed how the writings related to sex- and gender-based politics. Tim had been introduced to the *Communist Manifesto* in his girlfriend's commune. "At Skyline we tried to develop a Marxist version of 'the means of production,'" he recalled. "Marx talks about who owns the means of production: the land, the property, the mechanics, etc. ...how about the means of *reproduction*? ...You could see that much of the analysis Marx made around production could be transferred to reproduction. Men felt that they owned reproduction, i.e., the women, who produced. We began to understand men's domination of women and the need to keep them dominated."[32]

And if the men at GLF meetings had flunked Sexism 101, with the result that women soon disappeared, Skyline would commit itself to feminist principles and root out misogynistic talk and behavior in themselves. The men read and discussed works by Shulamith Firestone, Robin Morgan[33] and Charlotte Bunch, who was a member of the influential Furies radical collective in Washington. The Furies were focused on feminist theory and publishing. "We are angry because we are oppressed by male supremacy," proclaimed the Furies in the first issue of their eponymous journal,[34] and they tried to live their beliefs by separating themselves from men. Among the Furies' core beliefs: "Sexism is the root of all other oppressions." Likewise, "Lesbianism is not a matter of sexual preference, but rather one of political choice which every woman must make if she is to become woman-identified and thereby end male supremacy."[35]

Skyline members appreciated this radical thinking and began looking to the Furies as intellectual leaders and "comrades." "I think we in Skyline wanted to get stricter politics for men, as the Furies were doing for women," said Tim, who had met Furies-to-be Charlotte Bunch, Sha-ron Deevey and Joan Biren through his radical girlfriend. "We invited them over [to Skyline] so we could hear their political and philosophical ideas, what they were planning to do. I don't remember the meeting being that productive or having any follow-up."[36]

The problem with cultivating a relationship with the Furies was that they were not easily courtable, even among women. "They were a force to be reckoned with and didn't look kindly on the less radical lesbians," said activist Lilli Vincenz.[37]

To help prepare themselves to lead a revolution, the Furies practiced karate, read Trotsky, studied the Chinese and Russian revolutions, and researched women's history.[38] Jim had met some of them, and they "had absolutely no hesitation saying they hated men" and did not want to work with them.[39] In the latter part of 1971 the women were also busy preparing the debut of their journal, which appeared in January 1972. Still, Skyline members kept gently approaching the women as best they could. They even submitted an article for publication in *The Furies*. The women rejected the essay, which was about male privilege and the roles men could play in the women's movement.[40]

One Fury who apparently *was* courtable was Rita Mae Brown. About a year before her novel *Rubyfruit Jungle* made her a well-known writer, Brown was already a veteran of Radicalesbians in New York. But she tended to go her own way on political correctness. She later wrote of the Furies, "...even though I shared space with these women, I barely paid attention to them...They were serious, as in achingly intent. How I sat through those meetings without cracking jokes, I don't know."[41] Comfortable among gay men, she was known to visit Skyline and regale the men with her opinions and funny stories.[42]

Besides their interest in Marxism and feminism, the white men of Skyline also could learn more about what it meant to experience racism through their intimacy with Ted.[43] Altogether, Skyline seemed well po-sitioned to confront any sexist or racist impulses—in brief, to get more politically aware.

One result of this seriousness of purpose was a sense of isolation from their friends at the GLF commune. The residents of the two houses continued to visit back and forth, but Skyline seemed, to some residents of the commune, elitist, "uppity" and middle-class, all talk.[44] GLF was the fun house, Skyline the boring house.[45] Bruce Pennington, who lived at the GLF commune, recalled: "I had a feeling of not measuring up politically, that they were going on to something more profound and important…Skyline was definitely 'more revolutionary than thou.' "[46]

SOON SKYLINE HAD the opportunity to do something concrete: produce a nationally distributed magazine's special issue about gay liberation. *Motive*, published in Nashville, Tennessee, was a progressive monthly intended mainly for young adults, and was sponsored by the United Methodist Church. It combined politics, poetry and fiction with essays and reported articles, and took strong stands on civil rights and the war in Vietnam. Running out of funds, the publishers

Motive, 1972 (Artwork: Fag Rag)

decided to shut down the magazine and go out with a bang—the publication of two provocative editions, one devoted to lesbian and feminist issues and the other to gay men's liberation.[47]

 Motive staffer Roy Eddey was chosen editor of the issue on gay men. He met the men of GLF-DC through his work on the lesbian/feminist issue, which was produced largely by the Furies. "We clicked," he said, "as if we had been best friends for 50 million years."[48] Eddey decided to work largely with Skyline members to produce the issue because of their interest and discipline, and not least because Jim and David could provide design and typesetting services. After work, the two would stay behind and use office equipment to do typesetting.[49]

 In the opening essay of the issue, co-editors Ferri and Eddey linked their own struggles to those of lesbians. They described their emergence through coming out, joining consciousness-raising groups and embarking on a Marxian "personal/political analysis of our oppression." This analysis pointed them toward goals of ending male/female social-sexual roles, male chauvinism, racism and the sexual objectification of other men. The goal was challenging: "By destroying these masculinist traits in ourselves and confronting these traits in other gay men, we move toward 'de-manning' ourselves, toward giving up our male privileges, and toward ending our immediate oppression of Lesbians and ourselves."[50]

The issue included essays on coming out, organizing at colleges, imprisoned gays, and psychotherapy. Poetry—including works by New York activist Kenneth Pitchford—appeared throughout. Artwork and photography were provided by gay men and lesbians.

After many weeks of volunteer editorial and production work (I helped proofread the issue), the pages of *Motive* were shipped off to the printer in Atlanta. Whereupon the printer balked at some of the "indecent" artwork in the issue. The issue contains a number of fanciful and indistinct drawings of male nudes—with maybe one or two barely identifiable penises. Production was delayed for several months. When the magazine finally appeared in fall 1972, copies went to subscribers, university libraries and Methodist youth groups, as well as to gay bookstores in major cities.[51] With its limited distribution and the printing delay, the gay men's issue of *Motive* had less impact than it might otherwise have had. The content no longer seemed fresh in the changing currents of gay politics, according to editor Eddey. Still, the issue provided a snapshot of gay liberationist thinking up to 1972. And for Skyline, *Motive* was a proud achievement of collective editing, design and production. The men had made a magazine.

TOWARD THE END OF 1971, Michael and Kent noticed that fundraising jars for the Venceremos Brigade had been set out at the Community Bookshop, where they volunteered. They knew at once that they had another consciousness-raising job on their hands.

Set up in an old townhouse in the business strip just west of Dupont

Circle, the Community Bookshop, at 2028 P St. NW, was a countercultural hub in the neighborhood. It specialized in radical books, including fiction, and also sold periodicals, posters and buttons.[52] Its bulletin board posted housing, employment and meeting notices. There were meeting rooms upstairs. The 30 or so volunteers who worked at the bookstore were part of a collective, and everyone had to serve on one of the committees that made decisions about stocking and running the store. This radical retail operation was an experiment, and, as *Quicksilver Times* reported, "self-criticism sessions are constant!"[53]

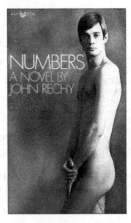

A Community Bookstore volunteer quashed this John Rechy novel as too objectifying.

Michael, Kent and other volunteers had stocked the store with gay literature.[54] They grouped the works of homosexual writers on a couple of shelves labeled "Gay Liberation," thus providing what was likely the city's first non-erotic gay books section—and a new way of seeing the works of homosexual writers. Like others, I was familiar with the standard "problem of homosexuality" books that libraries sometimes carried under Psychology, and I sensed the significance of the occasional Gore Vidal or Tennessee Williams title bobbing on the sea of literature. (I later discovered that the D.C. Public Library carried several novels, long since discarded, by Pierre Louÿs and Frederick Rolfe, works imbued with a refined fin de siècle gay sensibility—though in 1971 I had not yet heard of them.) But now at the bookshop, Vidal and Williams were part of an ever-expanding selection that provided readers with writings by current and long-gone "gay" writers—and a sense of forebears, individuals who had gone through experiences similar to mine, regardless of their isolation and lack of physical descendants. For me at least, the store's commitment to such works opened the window to a new concept—gay history.

Stocking decisions were political decisions. In a November 1971 dispute between the store and a Gay Ad Hoc Committee for an Improved Bookstore, "antigay" titles, such as anything by "homosexuals are sick" psychoanalyst Irving Bieber, were rejected in favor of more positive books.[55] Erotic fiction and magazines were considered inappropriate.[56] Jarratt returned John Rechy's novel *Numbers* to the publisher. The photo of an all-but-naked young man on the cover was a problem. He sent along a righteous note to the publisher asserting that the cover "was sexist and too objectifying."[57]

The Venceremos Brigade fundraising jars signaled that anti-gay forces were encroaching on a gay-friendly space. The brigade, an organization started in 1969, regularly sent groups of a few hundred people on two-month visits to communist Cuba to work side by side with Cubans—often in cane fields—in order to show solidarity with the Cuban revolution and learn firsthand about life in a revolutionary society. Organized in part by members of Students for a Democratic Society and Cuban officials, the group skirted U.S. travel restrictions to Cuba and attracted radicals of every stripe. By late 1970 gay liberationists were participating.[58]

But disturbing reports of entrapment and homosexual rehabilitation camps began to emerge. In May 1971 Cuba's First National Congress of Education and Culture clarified the situation with a statement criticizing the "pathological character of homosexual deviations." For offenders, the authorities would consider "preventive and educational measures" including relocation, and they backed "severe penalties" for those who corrupted the morals of minors and for "depraved repeat offenders and irredeemable anti-social elements." The official statement said homosexuality had the status of a disease, complete with stages, degrees of deterioration and contagion.[59]

Now that the Cuban position on homosexuality was clear, gay brigadistas could go to Cuba only if they decided not to be "gay first,"[60] that is, if they chose to hide their homosexuality and set aside the U.S. radical gay view that gayness was a step *toward* revolution. When a fifth brigade contingent was announced for February 1972, with applications available at the Community Bookshop,[61] one thing was apparent to radical gays: The brigade was implicitly supporting antigay brutality. Michael and Kent buttonholed a bookstore coordinator, who argued that bourgeois gay concerns would have to wait until after all other oppressed peoples in the world were fed, clothed and housed.[62] Michael and Kent decided some kind of action was needed.

Activist Kenneth Pitchford reads his poetry to a largely gay audience at the Community Bookshop in 1972. (Photo: David Duty)

On January 12, 1972, as Skyline members later wrote, about 25 "angry faggots" met with the Regional Brigade's coordinators and chosen brigadistas. (I went along, happy to be an angry faggot for the evening.) The protesters cited the Cuban resolution and read letters from Cuban gay people and from returned gay brigadistas telling of oppressive treatment there. The gays demanded the brigadistas withdraw from the brigade and make public their reasons. The response was not encouraging: Brigade supporters accused the gays of "cultural nationalism" and asked them to prove their "anti-imperialist credentials."[63] Some at the meeting, recalled Michael, said that gay people simply weren't oppressed. No one was persuaded to withdraw from the brigade.[64] The Bookshop collective members were supportive of the gays' demands but put off deciding what to do about the donation cans until the next community-wide bookshop meeting, which was about a week away.[65]

Skyline wanted to take action before then and decided to crash an upcoming fundraising party for the brigade.

It was fortunate that New York activist and poet Kenneth Pitchford happened to be visiting Skyline collective at this time, partly to help out in the *Motive* editing process[66] and partly to do a reading from his as-yet-unpublished collection of poems, *Color Photos of the Atrocities.*

Ken had already confronted the brigade in New York,[67] so he'd be useful at a Venceremos fundraiser. He was a member of the New York collective the Flaming Faggots, and while visiting Skyline he shared his political views on such subjects as misogyny and transvestism,[68] which would find formal expression when the Flaming Faggots later evolved into the Effeminists and published a magazine called *Double-F*.[69] Effeminism, as the movement was known, stated that misogyny runs through gay liberation. Effeminists believed that "all women are oppressed by all men," and that male supremacy produces sexism, racism, classism, ageism, economic exploitation, ecological imbalance and other forms of oppression.[70]

What can gay men do about it? They should struggle to rid themselves of male privilege. They should, for example, be politically militant without acting competitive and dominating; get in touch with their feelings; learn to give and take criticism; read feminist literature; start consciousness-raising groups; provide child care; eschew drag (which is considered antiwoman);[71] and attack male institutions such as the church, psychiatry, capitalism and the education system.[72] Effeminists should also avoid viewing other men as sexual objects, and avoid engaging in dominant/submissive role-playing.[73] Skyline was already earnestly working on or voicing support for some of these correctives.

Visiting Skyline, Ken freely opined on many things, for example, the inadvisability of two people living in a radical collective in an exclusive personal relationship (read Jim and David).[74] Jim recalled one evening when Ken criticized his concerns about housekeeping, then finally zeroed in on his beef stew. "He didn't like the dinner I made that night," Jim recalled. The stew "somehow became a way of mistreating everyone because I didn't consider them important enough to give something other than a hodgepodge meal." The evening's cook would have none of this criticism, and the discussion quickly became a shouting match.[75]

But Ken was also an accomplished and well-connected activist. Energetic and funny as well as passionate, he had the added cachet of being married to feminist writer Robin Morgan (a former child TV star from the popular early-1950s series *Mama*). Perhaps also because he was older, Skyline looked to the poet as a teacher, recalled Michael, and also— despite his sometimes hard-line radicalism—as an ally and a friend.

On Saturday, Jan. 15, the ad hoc "D.C. Faggots" attended a Venceremos fundraising party that was held at a Georgetown townhouse.[76] GLF activist Warren Blumenfeld worked at the National Student Association with the woman who hosted the party. She was a member of the brigade as well as a youngish Georgetown matron. Blumenfeld felt guilty about crashing his coworker's party without warning her, but political necessity came first.[77]

The 10 to 15 uninvited guests knocked, and, "when the door was opened we said, 'We're the queers,' and burst in," Jim recalled. Once inside, the men, some wearing bits of feminine attire, encountered a civilized hors-d'oeuvres-and-wine gathering.[78] "We want to struggle with you about the sexism of the brigade and the exclusion of gay people," the intruders announced. Several men made individual statements.[79] The group had also prepared a handout titled "Welcome to a Faggot Workshop" that explained why guests were being asked to withdraw their support of the brigade.[80]

The reaction of guests was mixed. Most of the pro-Cuban guests did not want to hear what the gays had to say, and there were a few angry exchanges. Others were polite and "patronizing."[81] But, as Jim recalled, some women "really came on our side, saying it was a chauvinistic, sexist operation, and support should be questioned until these men are accepted and their issues are dealt with." One regional coordinator resigned her position after the party.[82]

After a while, the exchanges devolved into chitchat. To Ken, the hostess seemed to be blasé about the gay invasion. Perhaps too blasé. Standing on a staircase, Ken heard a nearby young man ask his woman friend, "Why are these people complaining? People are suffering elsewhere." Ken had often heard that kind of talk before, in effect saying that his suffering wasn't really suffering. Frustrated, he shocked the young man—and himself—by grabbing him and kissing him on the lips. The woman friend then comforted the man, and others in the room called Ken's action brutal. "Well, that seems to have defused the whole evening," Kent observed, and indeed, after the kiss, there was nothing much else to say or do. The uninvited guests soon left.[83]

Back at work after the action, Blumenfeld managed to patch things up with his coworker. She went to Cuba as planned.[84]

National Venceremos officials stuck to their guns despite the dustup in Washington. A committee created a policy on gay recruitment stating in part "that Cuba's anti-homosexual policies were made by Cubans for Cubans; that homosexuality is for Cuba intimately linked with the decadent bourgeois culture that flourished when Havana was the sex and luxury capital of the Western businessman/politico"; that gay behavior by Americans in Cuba has in the past been "destructive" and "a flagrant insult to Cuban culture"; and "that the primary objective of the [brigade] is to show solidarity with the Cuban revolution."[85]

So there. But Skyline's action brought a victory, too. At the general meeting of the Community Bookshop, the collective members supported the Skyline Faggots. The bookshop would "refuse its support to the local contingent of the Venceremos Brigade by denying the Brigade its money and facilities until such time as the Brigade criticizes itself and Cuba in a real and meaningful way by word and action concerning the Brigade's and Cuba's oppression of gay men and women."[86]

SIX MONTHS INTO Skyline's collective living experiment, relationships began to sort themselves out, and it became evident that revolutionary self-criticism did not make for everyone's idea of a happy home.

The most obvious issue was that only five of the six men in the collective lived in the Skyline house and were actively gay. Tim Tomasi continued to live with his girlfriend while attending Skyline house meetings. Although the others supported Tim through his uncertainties, the "social acceptance" he enjoyed while seeming to live as a bisexual opened him to criticism. It took months of discussion before Tim was able to get to "my emotional as well as physical coming out."[87]

Kent Jarratt treasured the sense of family that Skyline provided, but his main goal was to write. "I just stayed up on the top floor and was the artiste and wrote," he said. In November 1971, he learned that his play, *Whale*, was to be produced Off-Off Broadway, and it premiered in New York at the end of the month. But after this celebratory moment, he struggled for the discipline to keep writing—especially in the face of an unacknowledged alcohol problem—and was distracted by undercurrents in the collective. He sensed conflict, and "I felt I was drowning in a lot of that; it was sapping my energy."[88]

Theodore Kirkland fondly remembered the emotional struggles of the house: "There were times when we'd literally close the door on Friday and said, 'We're not coming out until we've worked this out.'" But he had qualities that didn't play well in the group. For one thing, he sometimes made assertions, such as claims about his parents' professional accomplishments, that did not stand up to scrutiny.[89] Only much later did he admit to insecurities about coming from a modest background and going to school in a largely white, middle-class environment. He began to understand himself better as a black man, began to develop black friendships, and finally switched from dating whites to blacks.[90]

Jim Lawrence could be fussy. With his hardscrabble upbringing, he felt personally responsible for the orderly operation and financial solvency of the collective. He felt the men were setting an example about how gays could live together. At the same time, he was the highest wage earner of the group for a while, and he felt entitled to certain things. "I used to go into rages if someone drank all the orange juice during the night and I didn't have any in the morning before I went to work," he said. Dedicated to his job, Jim had little energy left over for emotional problems in the collective.

David Duty felt he'd been thrown into the deep end of the sexual politics pool. He wasn't even sure he was 100 percent gay: He enjoyed spending time with women and wondered if there was a sexual element to his enjoyment. He felt in a way he had "married young."[91] He and Jim discussed their relationship and even tried to date other men,[92] but David also felt jealous if anyone else was close to Jim. The message coming from others in the group seemed to be that a monogamous relationship such as theirs was not politically correct but was an imitation heterosexual marriage.[93] A self-protective, private man, David was seen by some in the collective as remote.

Michael Ferri was generous and caring, to the point where one time he invited a helpless old alcoholic man to stay in the house for a few weeks. "Somehow we were taking care of him," Kent recalled. Michael had cared for his mother when she had fallen into poverty in the last, desperate stages of alcoholism, so he had empathy for those with such problems. But he could admittedly be bossy and competitive.[94] Perhaps he had a vision, however incomplete, of what politically pure gay life should be and felt that everyone's personal behavior should toe the line. And sometimes he announced that his personal needs were not being addressed. One unmet need was the love and support of one man (a man he would meet later in life).

Whatever the reason, Michael called special meetings to resolve problems. And more and more, he came to focus on Jim and David as a problem. They kept mostly to themselves. Sometimes Jim, as he later admitted, didn't attend a house meeting. Confronted about their commitment to the collective, Jim and David insisted they were committed and wanted to stay.[95]

Jim began to feel that Michael was targeting him. Jim had little interest in soul searching or in the minutiae of political correctness. His natural bent was toward group activities such as producing *Motive*, or going to a dance or a political meeting.[96] To Jim it seemed that every little thing you did or said was judged politically—even gift-giving. He recalled giving Michael a calendar as a Christmas gift, and Michael "pointed out to me how chauvinistic some of the writing was…Michael Ferri and I used to butt heads constantly because I didn't go through the day worrying about the social and political ramifications of everything I did, and it appeared to me that he did."[97] Admittedly "anal-retentive," Jim was more concerned about turning off unused lights and turning the house thermostat down to save on heating. But somehow, to him, these mundane concerns would initiate a discussion about class struggle, which baffled him. He felt that "useless" struggles about "trivial" things were the real waste of energy.[98]

And the "isms"! "You almost had to prove yourself, that you were …dealing with your…sexism, chauvinism, beauty chauvinism," Jim said. "I'd never heard the term 'beauty chauvinism' before the Shenandoah weekend. It's basically human nature to be physically attracted to an attractive person."[99] Yet somehow this was politically impure. And it seemed the word "privilege" was thrown around like a weapon: "If you were not from the working class, you were a privileged person, and, by nature, sexist and chauvinistic."[100] Jim figured he had no control over his background.

By the end of March an emergency house meeting was called to resolve the Jim and David issue. Feeling forced to choose between Jim

After Jarratt, Lawrence and Duty moved out, a reconstituted Skyline included Tim Corbett (front row left), Will Balk (second row left) and original members Michael Ferri (front row right), Tim Tomasi and Theodore Kirkland. (Photo: Rainbow History Project)

and the collective, David announced that he chose the house and would stay to struggle on with the group. Hurt and upset, Jim said he was leaving to work things out for himself. The two would try to address their relationship problems somehow. (During this meeting Ted walked out without explanation—to go to the circus, it later turned out.) A couple of days later another meeting was held, and the others decided they wanted *David* to go.[101] They asked Jim to reconsider his decision to leave, but by now his mind was made up.[102]

Soon David and Jim moved to their own apartment. Jim stayed friendly with Skyline, but David kept his distance.[103] Within a few months, the two stopped living together. Kent moved out in August 1972, feeling guilty for abandoning the others.[104] Tim Corbett and Will Balk, who both were eager to join Skyline, replaced Jim and David. And Tim Tomasi, now a full-fledged gay man, finally moved in.[105] Skyline felt a renewed sense of cohesion.

IN LATE 1972, Skyline members were stunned to find themselves attacked in the nationally distributed—albeit obscure—*Double-F* magazine. In it, the Effeminists (formerly the Flaming Faggots: New Yorkers

Steven Dansky, John Knoebel and Pitchford) came out swinging against the many gay individuals who did not measure up to their approach to politics and life. They named names.

Pitchford criticized Michael Ferri and Roy Eddey for the "anti-woman" editorial they'd written for *Motive* magazine.[106] He also accused them of explaining that it was all right for them to criticize women openly and parody them by costume or mannerisms, "all because you claim to have the imprimatur of a very 'heavy' group of feminists," an apparent allusion to Skyline's would-be relationship with the Furies. "My only way to repair the damage done to me," Pitchford wrote, "is to shout your treachery from the house tops...I will hack away at any and all such examples of male bonding, whatever the cost...even should I be forced to stand alone in a solitude as vast as the lack of one male friend."[107]

Two Skyline members (Jarratt and Tim Corbett) had used pseudonyms in the *Motive* masthead, and Pitchford called them out for their cowardice. (A fair charge, though Kent was brave enough to wear a 1940s dress over jeans and a T-shirt to his temp job at the office of former U.S. Attorney General Ramsey Clark.) Finally, despite the bond Tim Tomasi and Ken formed over their shared involvement with women, Tim offended because "you actually tried to tell me recently that there really was a difference between Nixon and [presidential candidate Sen. George] McGovern." Shocking.[108]

Pitchford's broad swipe at gay collectives also seemed aimed at Skyline. He attacked the practice of Marxist study groups—"all as a means for further dramatizing themselves to each other and avoiding action...without any real concern for those faggots trapped in lives of unrelieved torment, trapped in jails or mental hospitals, raped by electric shock or brutalizing chemicals or brutal guards or straight inmates..."[109] In Pitchford's ultrahigh dudgeon, his vocabulary increased accordingly, as he churned out impressive combos like "heterosupremacy" and "straight effemiphobic sadomasculine homofascist masters."[110]

Why the attack? Michael guessed that Skyline had offended Ken at a party in New York celebrating the long-delayed publication of *Motive*, a party at which some Skyline men wore eye makeup (any kind of male transvestism is sexist, according to effeminist thinking). Years later, Ken did not remember any eye makeup incident. He did remember his own discomfort as he socialized with soon-to-be enemies: The *Double-F* issue was already typeset at the time of the New York party.[111]

Kill or be killed. As Pitchford later summed the situation up, "the aura of the day" was to criticize politically incorrect behavior in someone before he or she criticizes you.[112] Apparently the men of Skyline had not succeeded in destroying masculinist traits in themselves or "de-manned" themselves or given up male privileges fast enough for him. About a week after the *Double-F* magazine was put to bed, he began to have second thoughts about what he had written, but by then it was too late.[113] Michael especially was stung by the public nature of the criticism and felt that Ken should have "struggled with us" on whatever was bothering him.[114] After that, Skyline members and Kenneth Pitchford never spoke again.

After the *Double-F* attack, the men of Skyline continued much as before, living quietly with an emphasis on mutual support within the family and less focus on action in the community. Despite the occasional Sturm und Drang in house meetings, "it never damaged how we felt about each other," said Tomasi. When the owner of 1614 S St. put the house on the market, Ferri, Tomasi, Kirkland, Corbett and Balk moved together to Q Street.[115] By about 1975 Tomasi had returned to medicine full time and moved in with a man he was dating.[116] He eventually relocated to California, where he practiced occupational medicine. Balk got his own apartment. Michael decided it was time to start a new life in California, and Ted and Corbett went with him.[117] Ferri spent much of his career as a hospital coordinator for financial counseling. Kirkland later volunteered at the Inner City AIDS Network and helped start D.C. Black Pride, the nation's first such celebration, in 1991. Confronting his personal problems, Kent became a social worker in New York, where he worked with several LGBTQ organizations, managed a private psychotherapy practice, and taught clinical casework. Jim later started his own graphic design company. David got interested in computers, beginning with systems analysis, and then spent the rest of his career providing technical support and training for clients.

So Skyline Faggots ended. The experiment in radical gay living "gave us back a real big chunk of our spirits and our souls, and let us go from there and lead our lives," said Michael. The others, despite a few bruises experienced along the way, had to agree.

Motive, *1972 (Artwork: Fag Rag)*

CHAPTER 9

A Community Blossoms

I WAS TYPING AGAIN.

After five months of travel in Europe and the Middle East, I returned to Washington in October 1971 with little money and no place to live. But I was back among friends in the radical gay community, so I knew things would somehow work out.

And they did. The Skyline Faggots collective solved my housing problem by generously taking me into their S Street house, and Kent Jarratt let me stay in his top-floor room. I soon became an informal part of the "family"—sharing meals, shopping trips and social outings if not house meetings—so much so that, when more than one collective member asked me if I was interested in becoming an official member of the group, I said, sure, I guess so. At the end of the year, though, the men discussed me at a house meeting and voted no. I was stung, but finding space in a rooming house nearby, I made a new start and remained on cautiously cordial terms with the men of Skyline.

As for money, I took a job as a dishwasher-busboy at Old Ebbitt Grill downtown, thanks to GLFer Bruce Pennington, who waited tables there. But soon I decided that typing with a temp agency would be the perfect fit. My spelling was excellent; I wouldn't be tied to any one employer for long; and the assignments would be varied even if the work itself was mostly mindless. And mindless work meant my mind would be free to think about what to do with the rest of my life. First I had to revive my rusty typing skills. By February 1972, I was spending time at the K Street office of Tele-Sec Temporaries practicing in their testing area. It took weeks of repeatedly failing their typing test before I finally managed to qualify as a Junior Typist and begin my life as an office temp.

I was comfortable enough at my work assignments to flame a bit in my attire. I wore casual clothes with touches of skag drag, e.g. silk flowers pinned to my shirt, and a shoulder-strap purse with a gay button on it. I figured if an employer considered me too outré, I would just move on to the next assignment. In my "real" life I had a more dramatic street look—a long Dutch army coat (picked up at an Amsterdam flea market) topped with a short, boxy secondhand black fur cape that a friend gave me. The cape emphasized the Joan Crawford shoulder look even more than the army coat under it already did. Atop all this, my shagged hair and scraggly beard peeked out from under a purple felt cloche pinned with a bunch of fake cherries. At 6 foot 2—well, actually closer to 6 foot 4, since with my newfound wealth I was unable to resist a pair of platform shoes in maroon, navy and gray suede—I was an exotic creature that few would want to mess with. If not a gay revolutionary, at least I looked like one. I felt like a star.

BESIDES THE PLATFORMS, having money meant I could now move beyond the other necessities of life—movies, records, books— and indulge in the occasional restaurant meal or evening out at the bars. For many of us, the big dance bars were irresistible, filled with flashing lights, throbbing music, and wall-to-wall warm bodies reeking of cologne and cigarette smoke. But for a year or two, the dance bars were competing with more wholesome, politically correct and cheaper gatherings. In October 1971, George Washington University junior Allan Vick had applied for university recognition of a new Gay Liberation Alliance on campus.[1] Pennington, who was a part-time student at GW, helped get the organization started.[2] But Vick decided to model the new group only partly on GLF. He emphasized outreach, support and social functions because, as he said, "many gays are not militant and because, too often, militancy defeats the purpose of a movement by alienating the public."[3] The group soon changed its name to the Gay People's Alliance.[4]

In early December 1971 the group sponsored its first public dance in GW's Marvin Center ballroom. More than 400 men and women attended,[5] and after that success, dances became a repeated event there. The GW dances worked because of the convenient location, the music selection, the sound system, and the spacious dance floor. The public nature of these events added a dash of political boldness as gays in their going-out finery moved among straight students in the Student Union.

A spiffed-up warehouse on 13th Street became the GAA Community Center in 1972. (Rainbow History Project photos)

A few detractors were bound to show up. Steve Behrens remembered leaving a GW dance and running into a sneering acquaintance from high school in the hall. "He said something like, 'Well, *Steve Behrens*, I *thought* we'd see you here.'"[6] For the most part, though, the GWU gatherings were pure fun. As one activist remembered the spirit of the dances: "Sometimes, when a favorite song came on, we would spontaneously join together arm over shoulder, form a circle, and kick like Rockettes."[7]

Beginning in March 1972, the community had yet another venue. The Gay Activists Alliance spiffed up a warehouse in the 1200 block of 13th Street NW and dubbed it their Community Center. During the six months of the center's existence, GAA held regular dances there, and I went to several of these. One night, after spending most of the evening getting myself into full Value Village skag drag (dress, open-toed heels, satin shawl, dangle earrings and a choker, curled hair under a veil), I was finally ready at 11 p.m. I dropped a Darvon and a Valium to minimize anxiety and neutralize the pain of dancing in heels. Once there, I reveled in the attention a bearded drag queen deserves. Another night at the GAA center, dancers were crazed with pure physical excitement when someone began underlining the music with a tambourine and a police whistle. That evening we reduced dance to its elemental form: simply leaping, for joy, into the air.

BUT GRADUALLY, as a working adult once more, I sensed that my overextended, self-indulgent youth was ending and that my years of being "down-and-out" couldn't go on forever. The challenge of living on the cheap was both stressful and satisfying—I became quite skilled at frugality—but I knew that if I ever needed real help, a safety net waited somewhere below me in the form of middle-class parents. I also trusted that a reasonably successful, if unimagined, future lay somewhere ahead. If I was the beneficiary of what I later understood to be white male privilege, so be it. I was who I was.

My youth was ending literally: I seemed to be aging! In spring 1972, seeing the first traces of lines on my face and deciding that I had physically peaked at 26, I took action. Even though I hated sports, I decided that a little maintenance work was in order, and I joined the old YMCA at 18th and G streets NW, which was one of the few options available in pre-fitness center days. (Walter Jenkins, an official in the Lyndon Johnson administration, had famously been nabbed in the men's room there in 1964 being "disorderly," i.e., having sex, so the building had a notoriety that lingered.)

I was an odd gym bunny. I started my exercise program by running on the Y indoor track, with 10 plastic bracelets clittering on my arm and my long hair flying behind me. Eventually I began to relax a bit in the macho atmosphere. I decided I needed to build a little muscle because, having moved in fashion from the natural hippie look, to radical patched jeans and work shirts, to skag drag, I now needed discernible pecs to display beneath the tight synthetic shirts (worn partly unbuttoned) that were appearing in stores as the disco era approached. So I cautiously headed for the weight room. This was the province of older, scowling musclemen who ominously grunted the approaching climaxes of their reps as they worked the big weights. I tried to remain invisible as I began to exercise with little free weights. The alpha males took no notice of me. It soon became obvious, though, that mysterious rites of subtle body worship and locker-room display were part of the gym environment. This discovery at first seemed strange to me, since I was used to the forthrightness proclaimed at GLF. Before long, though, the interesting erotic subcurrents far outweighed my political reservations, and I became a regular at the Y. (In fact, the subcurrents were often barely sub: Some men continued the Walter Jenkins tradition, yet members got along, quickly learning what to see and what to ignore.)

AND OH, BY THE WAY, while I was blithely living the life of a working man and getting in shape, I didn't really notice that D.C.'s radical gay moment was passing.

The formal meetings of D.C. Gay Liberation Front had ended by July 1971, and the well-organized Gay Activists Alliance had largely taken over the local gay rights movement with carefully planned actions devised to help gays achieve more civil rights. Still, the GLF commune on S Street continued to identify itself as Gay Liberation Front. Many people still thought of themselves as GLFers. Political actions were still taking place, of course, but some were individual efforts, such as visits to local schools and lunchtime discussion groups at workplaces. In other instances, GLFers took part in protests organized by others, for example, a GAA-organized protest at the Iwo Jima Memorial.

VISITS TO HIGH SCHOOLS were important because teenagers were confused and ill-informed about what being gay meant. They would ask questions such as: "Do gay men wear dresses? Who plays the man or the woman during sex? Do you have a lot of sex? Why don't you become straight if you're unhappy?" Real live gays could dispel misinformation (and provide role models for closeted teens). But attempts at school visits were not always successful. Sometimes nervous administrators canceled arranged visits even from a well-established expert like Frank Kameny.[8]

Warren Blumenfeld, here proudly posing for a 1972 passport photo in his mother's striped turtleneck, made education about gay issues his life's work. (Photo courtesy Warren Blumenfeld)

GLF activist Warren Blumenfeld was invited to speak about gay liberation at a suburban Virginia high school around October 1971. Students assigned to find a guest speaker had located him through the National Gay Student Center (which he had founded). Because he was part of a genuine education organization, high school administrators considered him a "professional" gay and not a gay radical, and they approved his visit.[9]

Warren grew up in the conformist, fear-stoked McCarthy era. His parents, concerned that their shy 4-year-old was exhibiting homosexual behaviors, sent him twice a week to a psychologist for nine years.[10] At each session, the psychologist asked young Warren if there was anything in particular he wanted to discuss. "I invariably said no. ...I did not understand why I was there in the first place...For the next 50 minutes, the psychologist and I built model airplanes, cars, boats, and trains—so-called age-appropriate 'boy-type toys.'"[11]

"If I learned anything during my time with the psychologist, it was that I should cloak my expressiveness and my feelings," Warren recalled, "only to be resurrected during those rare but precious moments of solitude." As a result of all this vague therapy (at age 4, Warren hadn't a clue about "homosexual behaviors"), Blumenfeld became convinced that something was indeed wrong with him. One day when Warren was about 8, his father told him: "'When you wave, you *must* move your whole hand at the same time. Don't just move the fingers up and down like you're doing.'" His father grabbed the crying boy's arm and vig-orously demonstrated how a proper male waves. "'Of course the other children pick on you,' he said. 'You act like a girl.'"[12]

Warren discovered GLF in 1970 at San Jose (California) State Uni-versity. He moved to D.C. in January 1971. Despite his radical political experience, he was still cautiously coming out—he'd had only two sex-ual experiences in his life—and was so naïve that he was not sure there would even be any gay people in Washington. At his new job, his gaydar activated immediately when he met an openly gay coworker, who took him to the GLF commune. When Pennington opened the door draped with feathers, Warren declared, "I'm home."[13]

The Virginia high school administration canceled Blumenfeld's talk, but students protested that decision. In the end, Warren was allowed to speak onstage but was separated from students. "I could come into the auditorium, I would be onstage, and the board would be sitting in the first row as a block between me and the students," Warren recalled. "This is homophobia in action!" he declared, then announced to students that the administrators had set up "a deflective shield to protect you from catching the virus of homosexuality." The students cheered him.[14]

Activist Cade Ware, seated center, was among those arrested at a GAA demonstration at the Iwo Jima Memorial. (Photo: Washington Star *Collection, D.C. Public Library)*

A JANUARY 1972 GAA protest at the Iwo Jima Memorial in Arlington was well planned, with reporters and photographers notified in advance. For months, in an effort to stop nighttime sexual activity there, the U.S. Park Police had stepped up undercover operations near the statue of the Marines erecting Old Glory in World War II, using attractive young plainclothesmen to lure and then arrest more than 60 men on morals charges.[15] Frank Kameny accused the police of enticement and beating homosexuals.[16] Capt. Paul Burgus of the Park Police rejected these charges and said, "From what I understand, you just have to walk down through there and they grab you."[17]

Park Police informed protesters approaching the memorial that they could not demonstrate on federal property without a permit, then gave them 15 minutes to leave the area. The gays were faced with the iffy task of defending homosexual sex at a Marine memorial. They decided to read a statement maintaining that this was "the unharmful activity of consenting adults, that heterosexual men and women have sought privacy to make love in wooded areas since the days of Adam and Eve, and that the police could spend time and money to better advantage protecting us all from rapists, muggers, pushers and thieves."[18] The protesters then chanted slogans and marched to the monument.[19]

GLFers Bill Taylor and Joseph Covert took part, and they were arrested along with four others. When officers attached plastic handcuffs to his wrists, Taylor "just stuck my arms out and told everybody they could take a picture of that." The published photo of Taylor in skag drag with his arresting officer looks as if there

GLFer Bill Taylor is arrested at the Iwo Jima Memorial. (Photo: Washington Star *Collection, D.C. Public Library)*

were no hard feelings on either side. In the police wagon, when an officer kept looking back at the two arrestees, Taylor, happy to shock, said, "Joe, kiss me!" and Covert complied with a big kiss on the lips.[20] (Sadly, the monument was the site of a murder in October 1976, when a 32-year-old married father from Springfield, Virginia, was beaten to death there. Park Police had backed off after the 1972 protests, but after a series of beatings and before the murder, the Mattachine Society had asked the Park Police to step up uniformed patrols of the area.)[21]

MAY 1972 WAS a big month for local gays. Suddenly, we were legal!—or at least decriminalized in Washington. The case had started in 1970 when GLF activists stepped forward to declare their active homosexuality as plaintiffs in a case challenging D.C.'s sodomy law. The new sodomy ruling came at a good time. It was happily coincidental that gays here had already decided to celebrate with the first D.C. Gay Pride Week.

New York's Christopher Street celebration of 1970 had not only inspired D.C. gays to get a local Gay Liberation Front started but also ignited gay pride celebrations in big cities around the country.[22] Now, two years later, D.C. gays decided it was time to stage their own party. Gay Pride Week, May 2-7, 1972, was an ambitious attempt to be all things gay to all gay people. With activities around the city and beyond, this predecessor of Capital Pride was literally all over the map. Unlike the block parties and street fairs of later Pride celebrations, the first Gay Pride Week had no parade, no street festival, no corporations eager to declare their friendliness. Organized largely by GLFers Pennington, Cade Ware and Chuck Hall,[23] Gay Pride Week was "a celebration of our own community. We are a wide variety of human profiles and backgrounds—women, men, blacks, whites, leather people, drag people, conservatives, revolutionaries, Aquarius children, devotees of establishment lifestyle."[24]

Kicking off the activities at the Community Bookshop on P Street was a five-day series of events including an arts and crafts show, rap sessions, and a poetry reading featuring local poet Ed Cox.[25] On the evening of May 2, I attended the "Rhinestone Review," put on for free at GW's Marvin Center by the Henry Street drag organization.[26] With knowing nods to Broadway musicals and old movies, performers lip-synched numbers from *Dames at Sea* and *Cabaret*, and did amusing take-offs on the Andrews Sisters and Shirley Temple. One drag queen stripped.

At noon on Friday, May 5, I was happy to participate in a "public display of affection" in Lafayette Square with about 50 other men and women, a rally "to help end the stigma and oppression homosexuals say they have met,"[27] as the *Washington Post* put it. Gathering in the square across the street from Nixon's White House, the demonstration included speakers Rich Wandel, president of the Gay Activists Alliance of New York; the Rev. Robert Clement of the Church of the Beloved Disciple in New York; and Merle Miller, author of the 1971 memoir *On Being Different*.[28] I don't remember any immodest displays of affection. I guess we were supposed to hug and kiss one another for shock value, but we mostly sat on the grass politely listening.

That night, I was wide awake. At midnight, the new, all-male Metropole Cinema Club,[29] at Fourth and L streets NW, was offering "free gay movies" for both men and women, as part of Gay Pride, so a bunch of us went, curious and mildly titillated about being in an adult movie theater. I'm not sure what we were expecting—after the day's activism, perhaps some soft-focus gay-is-a-very-beautiful-thing dream—but the films did make an impression.

The lesbian shorts were stag movies, straight male fantasies. One of the cheapos—with no soundtrack—involved two women dressed only in stockings, garter belts, G-strings and spike heels. As the two engaged, we in the audience watched, also silent but stunned. The male feature was about hustlers in Hollywood and presented fake interviews in which the actors asked questions like "What was your most lucrative trick?" and "How do you handle weirdoes?" The answers were then reenacted. One scene involved a classic seduction: Hustler No. 1 is discovered having an erotic dream by Hustler No. 2. Then lots of beer drinking and saying things like Christ I'm horny. Shit but it's hot in here. Man, these pants are tight! The usual guy talk. Finally, No. 2 reaches for No. 1's crotch, and away we go!

Feeling (albeit belatedly) embarrassed about watching the porn, I bolted from the theater before the feature was over only to find GLF friends in the lobby having anxiety attacks about the presentation: Offensive! Objectifying! Oppressive!

The lineup of a dozen workshops and seminars offered at All Souls Unitarian Church on Saturday, May 6, got back to serious subjects. It included discussions of gay youth; gays in prison; media coverage; gays and the military; religion; the need for gay studies; Third World gays; legal and health issues; and the role of gays in presidential politics.[30] The Gay Activists Alliance sponsored an arts festival at its community center and held a free dance there on Saturday.[31] At a Sunday picnic in Rock Creek Park, some of the men in a game of volleyball stopped playing because others were being too competitive, which apparently made them feel oppressed.[32] Finally, a vigil in support of gay prisoners was slated for May 7 at Patuxent State Prison in Jessup, Md.[33]

After this first Pride celebration, the idea of GLF largely dissipated, but not before former GLFers helped start several surprisingly durable support groups and businesses. None sprang up purely through GLF, but all had significant GLF input, inspiration or ties. And those who helped start these services used the build-it-and-they-will-come approach that had worked at the GLF commune. Among these were Lambda Rising bookstore, Whitman-Walker Health, the Metropolitan Community Church of Washington, and the Gay Men's Counseling Community.

Deacon Maccubbin organized the first Gay Pride Day in 1975 (seen here holding plaque, with Kameny, left, and D.C. Council member John Wilson) and opened Lambda Rising bookstore. (Photo: Rainbow History Project Digital Collections)

TALL, BEARDED L. Page "Deacon" Maccubbin had antiwar hippie creds to spare. In the late '60s he publicly burned his National Guard reporting papers and was restricted at Fort Belvoir for several months as a result. He later hawked *Quicksilver Times* on the streets of Georgetown.

As an incipient gay man, Deacon felt almost none of the trepidation that many other gays had experienced. At 18 he suddenly noticed—in a new way—a college friend who sometimes spent the night at his place after parties. One morning, after a party, Deacon awoke early and observed his friend asleep across the room, with the sun falling across his skin through the blinds, the sheet halfway down his body, and golden curls falling on the pillow. "I thought to myself, 'Wow, I really want to have sex with this guy! I want to make love to him.' Then I thought, 'What am I thinking?' It was really a shock to me to be thinking that way, because up to that point I hadn't. But nonetheless, having realized what I wanted, I set about to see if it was possible."[34] He later came out publicly during a Unitarian church service. In D.C. he attended GLF meetings but gradually decided that direct action, not discussion, was the political mode best suited for him.

A business opportunity presented itself that allowed him to apply his singular self-confidence to a retail experiment. In 1972 he bought a consignment shop at 1724 20th St. NW for $100 and opened Earthworks, a tobacco and head shop, in the space. Later he introduced books there, and before long Lambda Rising, D.C.'s first stand-alone gay bookstore, opened in 1974. The expanding store later moved around the corner to S Street and still later to a prominent location on Connecticut Avenue. After many successful years, Maccubbin closed the store in 2010.

The bookstore's original location on 20th Street was a counter-cultural center that at various times housed a free clothing exchange, a theater, an anticapitalist record store, a gay youth group, the Black Panther Defense Committee, the Drug Offenders Rights Committee, the Washington Area Free University, Off Our Backs collective,[35] and the Gay Switchboard collective.[36] Maccubbin was a member of the D.C. Switchboard collective, which provided information on the draft, abortion, legal counseling, jobs and housing.[37] He saw the growing need for a specifically gay information line and helped get it started. When it opened in November 1972, Gay Switchboard provided much of the information—about bars, VD services, legal advice, social events, organizations and rap groups[38]—that the GLF commune had offered informally. Now, trained volunteers staffed an operation that ran seven nights a week. Some calls involved crises;[39] some callers just needed to connect with another gay person. One young gay man found GLF volunteer Bill Taylor when he was about 15. "I called the operator and asked her for gay anything, a hotline," he said. "[Bill] was a Wednesday evening operator. I would call him every Wednesday."[40]

In 1975, Maccubbin rethought the structure of 1972's Gay Pride Week and started Gay Pride Day. This time the event had one location, on 20th Street near S, by his bookstore. Music, tables set up for distributing information, and appearances by local politicians made the event a draw. Within a few years, the celebration outgrew its location and ultimately evolved into Capital Pride.

TODAY'S WHITMAN-WALKER Health had its roots in gay volunteerism at the Washington Free Clinic. The clinic, whose mission was to support anyone needing medical care, began operations in the late 1960s with a large core of volunteer doctors, nurses, psychiatrists, psychologists, clergymen, social workers, medical technicians and pharmacists.[41]

It operated out of the basement of Georgetown Lutheran Church (on Wisconsin Avenue at Volta Street), testing and treating clients at low or no cost. Many impoverished young people used the clinic for medical care.

By the summer of 1972,[42] with many sexually active young gays needing medical attention, the Saturday afternoon men's clinic had become an unofficial Gay VD Day at the clinic. A number of volunteers from GLF worked at the clinic, keeping records, performing simple medical procedures. Once you got past the sign-in table, you waited to enter a warren of "examining rooms" constructed out of sheets hung up for a bit of privacy. The volunteer in this space might be someone you knew from the community, but here he got to know you much better, as he took swabs from throat, penis and rectum, as well as blood. Exposing yourself completely to a peer was embarrassing and reassuring at the same time. A VD test at the clinic was encouraged as a social duty, to make sure you hadn't contracted or spread gonorrhea or syphilis. For some people it was also a social occasion. As Pennington remembered Saturday afternoon clinic visits: "If you were lucky, you met somebody nice there and went to the Georgetown Grill and had drinks and maybe had a date for the evening."[43]

By the end of 1973 a small group calling itself the Gay Men's VD Taskforce began discussing what could be done about the "VD epidemic" among Washington gay men.[44] Some 36,000 cases of venereal disease in the Metro area general population had been reported in 1972, with perhaps four times that number going unreported; area officials began a campaign to educate young adults about gonorrhea and syphilis and to encourage testing.[45] The taskforce soon officially established the Gay Men's VD Clinic at the church.[46] In 1977 the GMVDC separated from the Washington Free Clinic, regrouped, and in 1978 opened as the Whitman-Walker Clinic.[47] So Washington had developed a free medical resource for gays long before AIDS arrived in the early 1980s.

THE METROPOLITAN Community Church of Washington was founded by a GLFer, Paul Breton. As a young man aspiring to the Catholic priesthood, Breton had been unceremoniously dismissed from St. Bernard's Seminary in Rochester, N.Y., in 1964. He suspected the reason was

The Rev. Troy Perry, founder of the Metropolitan Community Church movement, speaks to the media at St. Stephen and the Incarnation Church, with Frank Kameny listening. (Photo: Dirk Bakker)

because he had openly questioned the expulsion of a classmate suspected of homosexuality.[48] Breton then served in the U.S. Air Force, but after military service he did an about-face and became involved in antiwar activities. And it was only at this point that he realized he was gay.[49]

Organizing wherever he saw a need, Breton created the Homophile Social League in Washington in early 1970 to provide casual social activities for gay people outside the world of bars.[50] Out of the HSL Breton started what became the nondenominational Community Church of Washington, with himself as a kind of moderator. "I just wanted it to be a forum through which we would have clergy and nonclergy from different religious groups come and talk and address the whole issue of homosexuality and religion," he said.[51]

In February 1971, the Rev. Troy Perry, charismatic founder of the Metropolitan Community Church movement in Los Angeles,[52] visited D.C. in part to speak at a Community Church of Washington service, which would also include the "holy union" of a gay male couple.[53] Anticipating a large turnout for the event, Breton asked the Rev. William Wendt of St. Stephen and the Incarnation Episcopal Church off 16th Street if he could hold the service there. Permission was granted. But when the nature of the event became known to William Creighton, bishop of Washington, Rev. Wendt had to uninvite Breton.[54]

Wendt informed Breton that the church doors would be locked. He also, "with a gleam in his eye," told Breton that the church had a side porch. Taking the hint, Breton held the Community Church service in freezing weather on the porch, with reporters and photographers in attendance. During the service, as the *Washington Post* reported, Troy Perry said, "Even though [Bishop Creighton] has locked us out of this church, God hasn't locked us out of His heart."[55] After the service the worshipers drove to the National Cathedral for a "kneel-in." At the altar, in a stage whisper, Perry began praying for homosexuals, heterosexuals and bisexuals.[56]

Denied the use of St. Stephen's Church for a gay wedding, Paul Breton conducted a Mass on the church porch in 1971. (Photo: Dirk Bakker)

Breton was impressed with Perry's take-charge, theatrical style. Perry was clearly on a mission, and he wanted to start an MCC congregation in Washington. Breton said he was "willing to do my part to help support and sustain at MCC but I was not at that time willing to be the minister." Perry prevailed, and almost before Breton knew what was happening, he was licensed a minister in MCC and was pastor of the brand-new church. Breton soon bought a Capitol Hill row house at 705 Seventh St. SE and began holding MCC services there. In May 1971 MCC dedicated the chapel. About 30 people attended,[57] sitting on the living room floor[58] and singing songs such as "The Times They Are a-Changing."[59] In 1973 Breton moved to an MCC position in another city.[60] The Washington MCC congregation continued to grow in borrowed spaces until in 1992 it built its own church at Fifth and Ridge streets NW.[61]

Both MCC-DC and the Community of the Love of Christ, which held services in the GLF commune, were serving D.C. Christian gays months before a chapter of the Roman Catholic group Dignity was established here in 1972.[62] In short order, various other gay religious groups formed, heralding the gradual acceptance of LGBTQ people by mainstream religious denominations.

RAP SESSIONS WERE ubiquitous in the early '70s, and informal opportunities to talk about gay issues were organized at the GLF commune, churches and elsewhere. The Gay Men's Counseling Collective (later the GMC Community)[63] grew out of the Washington Free Clinic's rap groups, which brought together professional therapists and volunteers to create a mentored corps of peer counselors.

The collective began individual counseling in February 1973. Membership was small, and counselor-member applicants had to undergo screening and a trial work period.[64] "We put ads in the paper," collective member Michael Ferri recalled. "A team of two of us would meet with the person and talk with him, and it was free...It was all very community-oriented, grassroots stuff.[65] " The GMCC later added group counseling and couples workshops.[66] Today, the GMCC continues to help gay men achieve "personal growth."

WASHINGTON WAS going gay. More and more groups sprang up to serve the city's diverse gay population. By 1973, a sampling of organizations included the Blind and/or Deaf Gay Group, Gay Alcoholics Anonymous, the Gay Women's Open House, Gay Youth, the Washington Area Gay Community Council, plus gay student groups at area universities.[67] With increased visibility, it felt like the larger straight world had at last come to some accommodation with gays' existence. In fact, as the *Washington Post* reported in 1973, "homosexuals rank Washington at or near the top among U.S. cities in terms of personal freedom."[68] Now, we had "gay neighborhoods," meaning the percentage of gays living in them was sufficient to ensure that gays could comfortably walk down the street hand in hand. The Dupont Circle area had long attracted gays, and now gays began to settle down in the area.

The *Post* also reported that "Washington's gay bars are owned by gays" and that most bars attracted a "mainstream" crowd while others catered to groups that "tend to segregate themselves": women, blacks, transvestites and leather.[69] (It's hard to know just how voluntary this "self-segregation" was, considering the sorry history of discriminatory gay-owned bars.) Oddly, there would be no gay bars in the Dupont neighborhood until Mr. P's opened in 1976. Still, for many of us middle-class whites living in Dupont, it seemed like we had reached Oz.

AMID THIS ASCENDANT gay scene descended the Divine Miss M herself. Bette Midler provided a kind of coming-out party for the community—and a blessing for gays—at her sold-out March 1973 concert at the Kennedy Center Concert Hall. This was to be D.C.'s first opportunity to come face to face with the new diva. We already knew she had come up out of the Continental Baths in New York. And we were prepped for her concert, since her *Divine Miss M* album had been released four months earlier, and we'd been devouring it.

Bette Midler: Relax, guys!
(Photo: Wikipedia)

Bette had quickly joined the gay pantheon. Now, with the recently anointed Liza (whose film *Cabaret* played at the Janus Theater for a year),[70] we had two brash new divas who drew their inspiration from 1930s and '40s showbiz. Both had transformed from ordinary-looking young women to stars through talent, style and smarts. One traded on emotional vulnerability, the other on bawdy fun. If Liza knew what we were feeling, Bette knew what we had been up to some nights. After all, at the Continental, only towels separated her from some basic facts of gay male life.

In D.C. everyone who had a ticket—gay or straight—seems to have decided that this concert called for something especially dressy. I restrained my more creative impulses this time and wore male attire plus a gleaming metalwork shawl borrowed from a friend. Oh, and curled hair and makeup. For Michael Ferri, it was time to declare: "Here we are, world! ...I got me all dressed up in those high-heeled dance shoes we were wearing in those days, wobbling a little bit. I fluffed my hair up and put on all sorts of jewelry."[71] Warren Blumenfeld decided, for his first time in "full drag," to come as his own version of Mamie Eisenhower, "with a blue-and-white polka dot dress, bowling shoes, a muff, and a hat with a veil."[72]

The elegant Kennedy Center was only a year and a half old,[73] so, as a *Washington Star* writer put it, "the august, monumental halls of the Kennedy Center never have seen such an unbelievable outpouring of the Washington gay community."[74] People fell back to gawk or applaud as the most outrageously attired attendees made their entrance into the Concert Hall. The show was delayed for almost half an hour while the audience enjoyed the spectacle of itself before finally settling down.[75]

"Aurora Borealis" (the ubiquitous Pennington), accompanied by "Andromeda" (Deane Bergsrud), made a sort of mother-of-the-bride entrance by proceeding slowly down the aisle to seats in the front row. (They had inquired about tickets before the show was even announced.) The two were in haute skag-drag. Bruce, according to reporters covering the event, was in "a hat that looked like a shower cap gone amok, but mustached and bearded,"[76] and also wearing "a tie-dyed caftan, green nail polish, faux emeralds pasted on his forehead, and green eye shadow." Deane was in a complementary outfit mostly in blue.[77]

When Miss M finally appeared, Bruce handed her an appropriately tacky boxed orchid corsage he had brought along.[78] Finally the Bette show began. This jiggling showbiz doll could do no wrong. We cheered her costumes, we screamed at her lewd jokes, we exploded little champagne-bottle confetti poppers, we waved our arms and danced to songs like "Chattanooga Choo-Choo" and "Chapel of Love." (It was not a good night to usher or clean the Concert Hall.) " 'I know what you've been thinking,' Midler said at one point, to a roar of approval. 'Oh divinity, where have you been all these months that we've been waiting here for you in D.C.?' "[79]

Indeed, and why such an explosive welcome from us? Finally, after all the Sturm und Drang of GLF meetings, the anger over bar discrimination, the hand wringing about the dearth of blacks, and the guilt over disappearing women, we'd found our new best friend forever. Camping, dishing and in general throwing outrageous attitude, Bette validated gay male life minus most of the politics. She had arrived, and the GLF crowd was happy to be swept along with her success. The Divine One seemed to be telling us: Relax, guys, have a little fun, not to worry so much about serious issues!

And gay men, at least, *were* easing back and moving on. Activism requires time and dedication, and now people developing careers seemed to have less of both. People were settling down, decorating apartments and entertaining. For many, the bar scene, with its promise of Dionysian intoxication and release, and maybe love, became the centerpiece of their social lives.[80] The few who kept the flame of radicalism alive tended to move on to cities such as San Francisco and New York.[81] As Blumenfeld summed up the change: "By '73, people who were counterculture were now in their business suits, and the transformative nature of the movement was dead."[82] (He later wrote extensively on gay subjects and taught at Iowa State University and the University of Massachusetts at Amherst.)

SO, HERE WE ARE, 50 years later. LGBTQ Americans have made great strides since the 1960s. A May 2018 survey released by the Human Rights Campaign Foundation reported, "Marriage equality is now the law of the land, transgender candidates are being elected to public office [let's not forget an openly gay presidential candidate], and mainstream television and movies routinely feature LGBTQ characters portrayed in a positive light."[83]

But problems persist.

The survey, released almost half a century after the brief existence of GLF, found "significant anxiety and fear among teenagers who identify as lesbian, gay, bisexual, transgender or queer."[84] These feelings included fears of being kicked out of homes, being sent for conversion therapy, bullying, rejection, isolation – complaints remarkably similar to those voiced in GLF in 1970. The survey did, however, report that young LGBTQ people with access to support systems were able to "mitigate negative experiences, reduce risky behaviors and lower distress."[85] In other words, the kind of support GLF began to provide in 1970, with consciousness-raising groups and other services, is essentially similar to what works today. Still, it's frustrating to know that prejudice continues and that each generation must face "otherness" anew.

In 1996, homophile pioneer Frank Kameny—who, among the many well-deserved honors he received toward the end of his life, had two blocks of a D.C. street named after him—dismissed Gay Liberation Front as "full of sound and fury…," without having to complete the *Macbeth* quotation. He told me he'd "had high hopes for something that could be utilized here as an extremely valuable tool…and it never came to pass." Setting aside the fact that GLF would not knowingly be Kameny's or anyone else's tool, it's true that noisy, disorganized GLF disappeared quickly. Its other detractors summed the group up several ways: "In trying to purge themselves of racism, male- and beauty-chauvinism, classism and capitalism, GLF members developed a multi-issue concern which spread their struggle thin over every conceivable political front," wrote activist Tony Jackubosky.[86] A disorganized organization, GLF never really had a conventional political agenda. One might even call the group, with its lack of political achievements, a textbook example of how not to have a revolution, a historical blip between the civil rights work of the Mattachine Society and that of GLAA.

But GLF was more than simply the shock troops of transition. At its peak, GLF attracted well over 100 participants to meetings, and those who came—firebrands, quiet organizers, those looking for love, kids along for the ride—somehow blossomed into a larger, supportive community where one had not existed before. What had been loosely connected, largely underground gay life suddenly blossomed into an open community in 1970.

One activist recalled, "I'd been fumbling around having a difficult time coming out, feeling fairly isolated. All of a sudden there was this whole community of guys and women who embraced me. It was a wonderful way to come out."[87] Tim Tomasi reflected that in participating in the movement—educating people, going to meetings, and talking to people about their individual and group oppression—he took his gayness "from being extraordinary to being a very ordinary part of my life." As D.C. journalist Tom Shales put it, despite GLF's failings, "for those who walked in out of the night air to those meetings, or made friends in the cell groups, or stood on street-corners handing out leaflets that said gay people are people too, 'gay liberation' may have been just that—the mere but important affirmation that what they are is what they are."[88]

As for myself, I drifted as an office temp for a few more years until I finally reentered the editorial world for good in 1977, beginning as a proofreader for Time-Life Books and building a career from there. As to gay liberation, receiving its gospel allowed a more or less whole gay person to emerge from a sick homosexual pervert. Did I move from inactivism to activism as a result of GLF? Hardly. Did I selfishly take only what I wanted from gay liberation and leave the rest? Yes. Did I trumpet my gay identity to the world? Seldom. But I was present when the tectonic plates of social norms were shifting, and I couldn't help but be moved.

Warren, Paul, Theodore, Jim and Tim. (Photo: David Aiken)

Timeline

1969

June 28: Stonewall riots begin in New York

1970

June 28: first Christopher Street Liberation Day, New York
June 30: GLF's first meeting in Washington, at Grace Episcopal Church, Georgetown
Sept. 1: GLF commune established at 1620 S St. NW
Oct. 17: GLF distributes "Are You a Homosexual?" handout
Nov. 11: GLFers zap a Catholic University seminar on theology and homosexuality
Nov. 14: gay dance at St. Mark's Episcopal Church, Capitol Hill
Nov. 27-29: Black Panther-sponsored Revolutionary People's Constitutional Convention; 12 GLFers are arrested after brawling at the Zephyr restaurant

---

1971

January-March: GLF pickets Plus One bar for discriminatory entrance practices
Feb. 3: Frank Kameny announces candidacy for D.C.'s new nonvoting delegate to U.S. House of Representatives
Feb. 14: Paul Breton and Metropolitan Community Church's Troy Perry hold a service on the porch of St. Stephen and the Incarnation Episcopal Church
March: GLF moves meetings to St. James Episcopal Church, Capitol Hill
ca. April: Nancy Tucker takes her leave of GLF with an angry letter
April: Gay Activists Alliance founded in D.C.
May: Metropolitan Community Church-D.C. established
May 1: May Day antiwar demonstrations
May 3: zap of American Psychiatric Association meeting
ca. June: Skyline Faggots collective moves into 1614 S St. NW
July: GLF meetings discontinued
September: Chapel of St. Francis and St. John established at GLF commune
October: Activists protest the Lost and Found bar's discriminatory entrance policies
October: Mattachine Society suspends regular meetings
December: first public gay dance put on by Gay People's Alliance of George Washington University

1972

Deacon Maccubbin begins selling LGBT books and magazines at his shop on 20th Street, which would become Lambda Rising bookstore in 1974

Jan. 5: Activists protest entrapment at Iwo Jima Memorial

January: "D.C. Faggots" confront the Venceremos Brigade over Cuban oppression of gays

March: GAA opens community center at 1213-1219 13th St. NW

May 2-7: First Gay Pride Week in D.C.

May 31: Sodomy decriminalized in D.C.

Fall: gay men's liberation issue of *Motive* magazine published

November: Gay Switchboard begins operation

December: Gay Men's Counseling Collective established

1973

March 11: Bette Midler concert at the Kennedy Center

Deacon Maccubbin's bookstore at its most prominent location, on Connecticut Avenue in the heart of Dupont Circle. (Photo: Wikipedia)

Notes

CHAPTER 1

1   Jean M. White, "Homosexuals Are in All Kinds of Jobs, Find Place in Many Levels of Society," *Washington Post*, Feb. 2, 1965, p. A12.

2   "The Hidden Problem," *Time*, Dec. 28, 1953, p. 28.

3   "Curable Disease?" *Time*, Dec. 10, 1956, p. 74.

4   "What Is a Homosexual?" *Time*, June 16, 1958, p. 44.

5   Warren J. Blumenfeld, "One Year Sick & Then Not: On the Social Construction of Homosexuality as 'Disease,'" blog posted February 2013.

6   Jean M. White, "Center to Treat Homosexuals Urged," *Washington Post*, Sept. 25, 1967, p. A3.

7   "The Homosexual: Newly Visible, Newly Understood," *Time*, Oct. 31, 1969, p. 61.

8   Sascha Segan, "Dupont Circle: Where Art and Eccentricity Meet," Washingtonpost. com, June 17, 1997.

9   Henry Allen, "The Ben Bow's Psychic Extremists," *Washington Post*, Oct. 2, 1971, p. C1.

10 Jean M. White, "Homosexuals' Militancy Reflected in Attacks on Ouster From U.S. Jobs," *Washington Post*, Feb. 4, 1965, p. A1.

11 Ann Devroy, "Clinton Overhauls Rules, Allows Gays Top Security Clearance," *Washington Post*, Aug. 5, 1995, p. A1.

12 U.S. Department of Defense questionnaire, probably 1970

13 Lillian Faderman, *The Gay Revolution: The Story of the Struggle*. Simon & Schuster, New York, 2015, p. 129.

14 Homophile Social League Newsletter, Vol. 1, Issue 11, Nov. 1, 1970.

15 "If You Are Arrested," *The Homosexual Citizen*, Vol. 2 No. 1, January 1967, p. 3. Courtesy of Lilli Vincenz.

16 Jean M. White, "Those Others: A Report on Homosexuality, *Washington Post*, Jan. 31, 1965, p. E1.

17 Lilli Vincenz interview by author, Aug. 15, 1998

18 From a Kameny letter to Larry Littlejohn of the Society for Individual Rights in San Francisco, Jan. 8, 1966, cited in *Gay Is Good: The Life and Letters of Gay Rights Pioneer Franklin Kameny*, edited by Michael G. Long, Syracuse University Press, Syracuse, N.Y., 2014, p. 120.

19 Eva Freund interview by author, Jan. 28, 1999

20 Patricia Hawkins Rainbow History Project oral history interview by Mark Meinke, May 22, 2009.

21 Lou Chibbaro Jr., "In 1969, D.C.'s Gay Life Was Already Thriving," *Washington Blade*, Oct. 7, 1994, p. 14.

22 Brett Beemyn, ed., *Creating a Place for Ourselves: Lesbian, Gay, and Bisexual Community Histories*. Routledge, New York and London, 1977, pp. 184-185.

23 Chibbaro, "In 1969, D.C.'s Gay Life"

24 Richard Lee, "The Gay Life," *Washingtonian*, Feb. 1970, p. 43.

25 Peter Jefts Rainbow History Project oral history interview by Allen Young, nd.

26   Lee, "The Gay Life"

27   Paul Kuntzler interview by author, July 28, 1998

28   *Washington Blade*, Oct. 6, 1989, p. 35

29   Rainbow History Project Places & Spaces database

30   "Hippie Culture Starts to Fray," *Washington Post*, Jan. 14, 1970, p. A1.

31   Charles A. Krause, "Cairo Hotel Getting Complete Overhaul," *Washington Post*, July 13, 1975, p. B1.

32   Lawrence Feinberg, "Jaded Cairo to Get a Facelift," *Washington Post*, Aug. 8, 1972, p. C1.

CHAPTER 2

1   One interviewee recalled attending a "GLF" meeting in August 1969, so it is possible that one or more exploratory meetings took place in 1969 or early 1970, but if so, apparently nothing came of them.

2   Lillian Faderman, *The Gay Revolution: The Story of the Struggle*, Simon & Schuster, New York, 2015, pp. 188-195.

3   *The Ladder*, Vol. 14, No. 1/2, Oct/Nov 1969, p. 39.

4   Lilli Vincenz interview by author, Aug. 15, 1998

5   *Gay Is Good: The Life and Letters of Gay Rights Pioneer Franklin Kameny*, edited by Michael G. Long, Syracuse University Press, Syracuse, N.Y., 2014, pp. 193-194.

6   "Radicals Mobilize to Take Over Homophile Movement," Liberation News Service, No. 195, Sept. 18, 1969, p. 17.

7   "A Radical Manifesto," North American Conference of Homophile Organizations, Aug. 28, 1969, Box 285073728 (Box 2 of 29), Renee Hanover papers, Lesbian Herstory Archives of the Lesbian Herstory Foundation Inc., Brooklyn, New York.

8   Nancy L. Ross, "Homosexual Revolution," *Washington Post*, Oct. 25, 1969, p. C1

9   Ross, "Homosexual Revolution"

10   Michael Yarr interview by author, Aug. 25, 1996; and the University of California Berkeley Library Black Panther chronology website backs his memory up: on May 1, 1970, a Black Panther rally in New Haven, Connecticut, drew about 12,000-15,000 (mostly students).

11   Yarr interview

12   D. Aiken, "Gay Liberation Comes to D.C.," *Quicksilver Times*, June 23-July 3, 1970, p. 4

13   *Gay Blade*, Vol. 1 No. 10, July 1970

14   Tim Tomasi interview by author, Apr. 11, 1995

15   Kameny letter to Anthony Grey dated July 3, 1970, quoted in *Gay Is Good: The Life and Letters of Gay Rights Pioneer Franklin Kameny*, p. 221.

16   *Gay Blade*, Vol. 1 No. 10, July 1970

17   Third World Gay Revolution split from GLF in New York in July 1970, according to the OutHistory website

18   Red Butterfly cell formed within New York GLF and began publishing materials by February 1970, according to the Pagan Press website

19   Morgan Pinney, "The Gay Liberation Movement in New York City," *Gay Sunshine*, Vol. 1 No. 4, December 1970, p. 2.

20   Jim Lawrence interview by author, June 11, 1994

21   Nancy Tucker interview by author, July 22, 2014

22   Joel Martin interview by author, Apr. 1, 1997

23 *Gay Blade*, Vol. 1 No. 11, August 1970
24 GLF Newsletter, Vol. 1 No. 5, Sept. 1, 1970, Frank Kameny papers, Box 92, Library of Congress
25 *Gay Blade*, Vol. 2 No. 2, November 1970
26 GLF Newsletter, Vol. I No. 13, Nov. 3, 1970, Box 285073726 (Box 1 of 29), Renee Hanover papers, LHA.
27 GLF Newsletter, Vol. 1 No. 12, Oct. 27, 1970, from Bruce Pennington papers, Rainbow History Project Collection, Historical Society of Washington, D.C.
28 GLF Newsletter, Vol. 1 No. 3, Aug. 18, 1970, Frank Kameny papers, Box 92, LoC.
29 Warren J. Blumenfeld, "One Year Sick & Then Not: On the Social Construction of Homosexuality as 'Disease,'" The Bilerico Project blog, Feb. 24, 2013.
30 Jim Fouratt interview by author, Nov. 21, 1998
31 GLF Newsletter, Vol. I No. 6, Sept. 15, 1970, pp. 3-4, Box 285073726 (Box 1 of 29), Renee Hanover papers, LHA.
32 Max Maynard interview by author, March 21, 1999
33 Thomas Shales, "Gay Liberation in D.C.," *D.C. Gazette* Vol. 2 No. 16, May 24-June 6, 1971, p. 4.
34 Temporary fact sheet for the Washington Gay Liberation Front (GLF Newsletter), no date (published Aug. 5, 1970), Frank Kameny papers, Box 92, LoC.
35 Paul Breton interview by author, Mar. 1, 2003
36 Temporary fact sheet (GLF Newsletter)
37 Nancy Tucker email to author, May 15, 2014
38 Homophile Social League Newsletter Vol. 1, Issue 11, Nov. 1, 1970
39 GLF Newsletter, Vol. I No. 6, Sept. 15, 1970, pp. 3-4, Box 285073726 (Box 1 of 29), Renee Hanover papers, LHA.
40 Martin interview
41 *Gay Blade*, Vol. 3 No. 9, mid-June 1972
42 Frank Kameny interview by author, May 11, 1996
43 Richard Schaefers interview by author, Apr. 29, 1996
44 Letter of Richard Schaefers to Insp. Walter Bishop, Aug. 21, 1970, courtesy Richard Schaefers.
45 Letter of Walter R. Bishop to Richard Schaefers, Aug. 31, 1970, courtesy Richard Schaefers.
46 Sanford J. Ungar, "4 Homosexuals Sue to Curb D.C. Police," *Washington Post*, Sept. 10, 1971. p. C2.
47 Bart Barnes. "D.C. Will No Longer Prosecute Private, Adult Homosexual Acts." *Washington Post*, 31 May 72, p. A1.
48 B.D. Colen. "Soliciting Statute Overturned." *Washington Post*, 2 June 72, p. A20.
49 *Gay Blade*, Vol. 3 No. 9, mid-June 1972
50 "Soliciting by Males Still Illegal," *Washington Post*, Apr. 20, 1974, p. D1
51 Rene Sanchez, "D.C. Sodomy Law Is Off the Books," *Washington Post*, Sept. 18, 1993, p. B3
52 Ungar, "4 Homosexuals Sue"
53 Kent Jarratt comments at a panel on Gay Liberation Front D.C. sponsored by Rainbow History Project and the Historical Society of Washington, D.C., June 7, 2014.
54 Warren Blumenfeld interview by author, Sept. 15, 1998
55 *Gay Blade*, July 1970
56 Bill Anderson interview by author, 5 Aug. 1998

57   Bruce Pennington interview by author, Dec. 29, 1994
58   *Gay Blade*, July 1970
59   Anderson interview
60   Brett Beemyn, ed., *Creating a Place for Ourselves: Lesbian, Gay, and Bisexual Community Histories*. Routledge, New York and London, 1977, p. 186.
61   GLF Newsletter, Vol. 1 No. 5, Sept. 1, 1970, Frank Kameny papers, Box 92, LoC.
62   GLF Newsletter, Vol. I No. 6, Sept. 15, 1970, p. 3, Box 285073726 (Box 1 of 29), Renee Hanover papers, LHA.
63   GLF Newsletter, Vol. 1 No. 14, Nov. 10, 1970, from Bruce Pennington papers, RHP.
64   GLF Newsletter, Vol. I No. 15, Nov. 17, 1970, Box 285073726 (Box 1 of 29), Renee Hanover papers, LHA.
65   Homophile Social League Newsletter, Vol. I Ed. X, Dec. 1, 1970, p. 15, courtesy Dirk Bakker.
66   GLF Newsletter, Vol. 1 No. 5, Sept. 1, 1970, Frank Kameny papers, Box 92, LoC.
67   Homophile Social League Newsletter Vol. 1, Issue 11, Nov. 1, 1970
68   Ned Scharff, "The New Radicals," *Washington Star*, Jan. 24, 1971, p. D7
69   "The Woman Identified Woman" by Radicalesbians. 1970
70   Kenneth Pitchford interview by author, Jan. 31, 1999
71   Tony Jackubosky interview by author, Nov. 11, 1998
72   Scharff, "The New Radicals"
73   John Maybauer interview by author, Apr. 28, 1999
74   Eva Freund interview by author, Jan. 28, 1999
75   Tucker email of May 15, 2014
76   Tucker email of Sept. 13, 2018
77   Nancy Tucker comments at a panel on Gay Liberation Front D.C. sponsored by Rainbow History Project and the Historical Society of Washington, D.C., June 7, 2014
78   Nancy Tucker interview by Rainbow History Project, Aug. 6, 2009
79   Tucker interview by author
80   Tucker interview by author
81   Tucker interview by author
82   Cliff Witt interview by author, July 21, 1998
83   The *Gay Blade* (essentially the writing of Nancy Tucker) early on used the word "girls." In the December 1969 issue she wrote, "Interested guys or girls can call the editors for info." In April 1970 she wrote, "He has married three couples, two of girls and one of guys." In the June 1970 issue she wrote, "Girls are strongly urged to come and make their voices heard."
84   Tucker email of Sept. 13, 2018
85   Tucker interview by author
86   Martin interview
87   Tucker comments on a panel on GLF, D.C., June 7, 2014.
88   Genny Beemyn, *A Queer Capital: A History of Gay Life in Washington*, D.C. Routledge, New York and London, 2015, p. 122.
89   James "Juicy" Coleman Rainbow History Project oral history interview by Mark Meinke, Aug. 20, 2001.
90   "The Clubhouse, Washington, DC," National Park Service information sheet, entry written by Amber Bailey for the Historic American Buildings Survey, from the Web, nd.
91   Will O'Bryan, "The Party Line," Feb. 13, 2008
92   O'Bryan, "The Party Line"

93   "The Buddy System," Otis "Buddy" Sutson interview by Sean Bugg, *Metro Weekly*, May 26, 2004.

94   Otis "Buddy" Sutson interview by the author, Sept. 8, 2018

95   "Gay DC Tours: African American," pamphlet written by Mark Meinke for Rainbow History Project, 2004.

96   GLF Newsletter, Vol. 1 No. 17, Dec. 8, 1970, Frank Kameny papers, Box 92, LoC.

97   Shales, "Gay Liberation in D.C."

98   Shales, "Gay Liberation in D.C."

99   Kameny interview

100 *Gay Sunshine* Vol. 1 No. 6, March 1971, p. 10.

101 *Gay Blade*, March 1971

102 Gay DC Walking Tours: South Capitol Street, pamphlet produced by Rainbow History Project, 2003.

103 *Gay Blade*, Vol. 3 No. 2, November 1971

104 Freund interview

105 Flyer "Woman Forcibly Ousted From Lost and Found," nd

106 Breton interview

107 "Fellow Gay People: Why Are We Picketing the Lost and Found?" undated handout from "the collective leadership of the Washington Gay Community," Rainbow History Project.

108 Flyer "Woman Forcibly Ousted"

109 "Gay People: Have We Come This Far Only to Leave Behind Some of Us?" flyer dated Oct. 23, 1971, from the Aiken papers courtesy Rainbow History Project.

110 "Off With Sexism & Racism in Our Gay Bars" flyer, nd

111 "Off With Sexism" flyer

112 "Gay People: Have We Come This Far...?"

113 Undated flier endorsed by GLF, GAA, University of Maryland Student Homophile Association, MCC, MSW, Evangelical Catholic Communion.

114 Lost and Found Classifieds, no date, courtesy Rainbow History Project

115 *Gay Blade*, Vol. 3 No. 7, April 1972

116 Patricia Kolar, "Discrimination Charges Against the Lost and Found," *Gay Blade*, Vol. 5 No. 2, November 1973, p. 5.

117 *Gay Blade*, Vol. 5 No. 4, January 1974

118 Rainbow History Project Places and Spaces database

CHAPTER 4

1   Various contemporary *Washington Post* accounts: even in 1978, junkies waiting for "the Candyman" were common at 14th and U, and further up the riot corridor (Florida Ave. to Spring Rd.), businesses faced junkies, robberies, unruly teens, purse snatchings and more.

2   Date per Redfin real estate website

3   William R. MacKaye, "Once-Thriving Commune Dissolves," *Washington Post*, Sept. 1, 1970, p. 29.

4   Carl Bernstein, "Communes, a New Way of Life in District," *Washington Post*, July 6, 1969, p. C1.

5   "Tim Corbett on the Gay Liberation Front House," from Friends Radio Program Records, digital collection, 1973-1982, Rainbow History Project.

6   Temporary fact sheet for the Washington Gay Liberation Front (GLF Newsletter), no date (published Aug. 5, 1970), Frank Kameny papers, Box 92, Library of Congress.

7   Bruce Pennington interview by author, Dec. 29, 1994

8   Theodore Kirkland interview by author, Aug. 12, 1994

9   David L. Aiken, "Dethrone the King," *Motive*, Vol. 32 No. 2, 1972, p. 48

10   Special Collections Finding Aid, Ms 0764, Historical Society of Washington, D.C. (the name has since changed to the Joint Center for Political and Economic Studies)

11   Bob Levey email, May 13, 2014

12   Thomas Shales, "Gay Liberation in D.C.," *D.C. Gazette*, Vol. 2 No. 16, May 24-June 6, 1971, p. 17.

13   Pennington interview

14   Nancy Tucker interview by author, July 22, 2014

15   Special Collections Finding Aid, Ms 0764 (Rainbow History Project Collection, Historical Society of Washington, D.C.

16   1986 *Washington Blade* obituary for David Aiken, nd.

17   Bruce Pennington community resume, Folder 38, Bruce Pennington papers, Rainbow History Project Collection, Historical Society of Washington, D.C.

18   Homophile Social League Newsletter. Vol. 1 Issue 11, Nov. 1, 1970

19   Michael Ferri interview by author, March 15, 2018

20   Bill Taylor interview by author, July 8, 1997

21   Pennington interview

22   "Tim Corbett on the Gay Liberation Front House," from Friends Radio Program Records, RHP

23   Pennington interview

24   Kirkland interview

25   Wade Carey interview by author, Aug. 15, 1996

26   Pennington interview

27   Paul Bartels interview by author, Aug. 9, 1998

28   Pennington interview

29   GLF Newsletter, Vol. 1 No. 5, Sept. 1, 1970, Frank Kameny papers, Box 92, LoC.

30   GLF Newsletter, Vol. 1 No. 9, Oct. 6, 1970, from Bruce Pennington papers, RHP.

31   Richard Lewis interview by author, Jan. 24, 2010

32   Ronald K. Fried, "How the Mafia Muscled In and Controlled the Stonewall Inn," *Daily Beast*, June 29, 2019.

33   Mike Yarr interview by author, Aug. 25, 1996

34   Bartels interview

35   Michael Ferri interview by author, July 24, 1994

36   Michael Ferri interview by author, March 15, 2018

37   GLF Newsletter, Vol. 1 No. 14, Nov. 10, 1970, from Bruce Pennington papers, RHP.

38   *Gay Blade*, October 1970; MSW balance statement 10 July 71.

39   GLF Newsletter, Vol. I No. 15, Nov. 17, 1970, Box 285073726 (Box 1 of 29), Renee Hanover papers, Lesbian Herstory Archives of the Lesbian Herstory Foundation Inc.

40   GLF Newsletter, Vol. 1 No. 3, Aug. 18, 1970, Frank Kameny papers, Box 92, LoC.

41   Carl Rizzi, Mame Dennis and The Academy of Washington Collection 6, Carl Rizzi papers, Rainbow History Project Collection, Historical Society of Washington, D.C.

42 Warren Blumenfeld interview by author, Sept. 15, 1998

43 Phil Herbert interview by author, March 3, 1996

44 "Sister" Brian Chavez, "Blatant Is Beautiful!" *Gay Sunshine*, Vol. 1 No. 2, October 1970, p. 9.

45 Carey interview

46 John Scagliotti interview by author, Feb. 15, 1999

47 Jim Fouratt interview by author, Nov. 21, 1998

48 Michael Ferri interview by author, July 24, 1994

49 *Gay Blade*, Vol. 2 No. 12, September 1971

50 Michael Ferri email, Feb. 24, 2018

51 Andy Hughes interview by author, Sept. 15, 1998

52 Metropolitan Community Churces website.

53 Online Lesbian, Gay, Bisexual and Transgender Religious Archives Network profile of Bishop Michael Francis Augustine Itkin

54 *Gay Blade*, Vol. 3 No. 10, mid-July 1972, p. 1.

55 Paul Breton interview by author, Nov. 17, 1998

56 Breton interview

57 *Gay Blade*, Vol. 2 No. 12, September 1971

58 *Gay Blade*, Vol. 3 No. 7, April 1972, p. 2.

59 The January 1974 *Gay Blade* makes no mention of the gay chapel or of the Gay Liberation Services House, so activities there would likely have stopped by the end of 1973.

60 Homophile Social League Newsletter, Vol. 1, Issue 11, Nov. 1, 1970

61 GLF Newsletter, Vol. 1 No. 2, Aug. 11, 1970, Frank Kameny papers, Box 92, LoC.

62 "On Our Own," *Motive*, Vol. 32 No. 2, 1972, pp. 50-51.

63 Mike Yarr interview

64 John Broere interview by author, Sept. 12, 1998.

65 Patrick Rosenkjar interview by author, May 11, 2018.

66 Blumenfeld interview

67 Liz Highleyman, "Past Out: Who Was Carl Wittman?" *Seattle Gay News*, Vol. 34 No. 18, May 5, 2006, p. 30.

68 Carl Wittman, "Refugees From Amerika: A Gay Manifesto, *San Francisco Free Press*, Dec. 22, 1969-Jan. 7, 1970.

69 Wittman, "A Gay Manifesto"

70 Steve Behrens interview by author, Feb. 25, 1996

71 Behrens interview

72 Behrens interview

73 Bill Anderson interview by author, Aug. 5, 1998

74 Frank Kameny interview by author, May 11, 1996

75 Vincenz interview by author, Aug. 15, 1998

76 GLF Newsletter, Vol. 1 No. 3, Aug. 18, 1970, Frank Kameny papers, Box 92, LoC.

77 Morgan Pinney, "The Gay Liberation Movement in New York City," *Gay Sunshine*, Vol. 1 No. 4, December 1970, p. 2.

78 Scagliotti interview

79 Tim Corbett interview by author, Aug. 14, 1994

80 Bruce Pennington interview by author, March 3, 2001

81 *Gay Blade*, Vol. 3 No. 7, April 1972

82   Bruce Pennington "personal data" and "community resumé," no date but after 1986, Folder 38, Bruce Pennington papers, RHP
83   Tim Tomasi interview by author, Apr. 11, 1995

CHAPTER 5

1   GLF Newsletter, Vol. 1 No. 10, Oct. 13, 1970, Frank Kameny papers, Box 92, Library of Congress
2   Temporary fact sheet for the Washington Gay Liberation Front (GLF Newsletter), no date (published Aug. 5, 1970), Frank Kameny papers, Box 92, LoC.
3   *Gay Blade*, October 1970
4   GLF Newsletter, Vol. 1 No. 11, Oct. 20, 1970, Frank Kameny papers, Box 92, LoC
5   Bill Taylor interview by author, July 8, 1997
6   GLF handout titled "Gay Liberation Front Inaugural Annual Merry Christmas Freak-out," Dec. 12, 1970, Box 285073726 (Box 1 of 29), Renee Hanover papers, Lesbian Herstory Archives of the Lesbian Herstory Foundation Inc., Brooklyn, N.Y.
7   GLF Newsletter, Vol. 1 No. 11, Oct. 20, 1970, Frank Kameny papers, Box 92, LoC
8   "Street Work," Homophile Social League Newsletter, Vol. 1 Ed. X, Dec. 1, 1970, p. 4, courtesy Dirk Bakker.
9   "Homosexuality Seminar Explores Attitudes, Stresses Social, Theological Implica-tions," *The Tower* (Catholic University), Nov. 20, 1970, p. 3
10   "Homosexuality Seminar Explores Attitudes."
11   Phrases extracted from "Marriage and the Homosexual" chapter in John R. Cavanagh, *Counseling the Invert*, Bruce Publishing Co., Milwaukee, 1966
12   "Gay Power Faces Down 'Doctor' Cavanaugh." *Quicksilver Times*, Nov. 24-Dec. 4, 1970, p. 5
13   "Homosexuality Seminar Explores Attitudes."
14   Cavanagh, *Counseling the Invert*, p. 223-224
15   Richard Pearson, "John R. Cavanagh, Catholic Layman, Prominent Psychiatrist, Dies at 76," *Washington Post*, May 4, 1981, p. C4
16   Cavanagh, *Counseling the Invert*, p. 256
17   "Workshops (Male Homosexual)," *Quicksilver Times*, Nov. 24-Dec. 4, 1970, insert
18   Lilli Vincenz column, *Gay*, Vol. 2 No. 40, n.d. [ca. Dec. 20, 1970]
19   GLF Newsletter, Vol. 1 No. 15, Nov. 17, 1970, Box 285073726 (Box 1 of 29), Renee Hanover papers, LHA
20   GLF Newsletter, Vol. 1 No. 15, Nov. 17, 1970, Renee Hanover papers, LHA
21   GLF Newsletter, Vol. 1 No. 15, Nov. 17, 1970, Renee Hanover papers, LHA
22   Michael Bernstein, "Homosexual Leader Hits Church," *Washington Daily News*, Nov. 10, 1970, p. 5
23   "Letter from Franklin Kameny—D.C. uproar," Chicago Gay Alliance Newsletter, Vol. 1 No. 1, December 1970, p. 5. Box 2850732728 (Box 2 of 29), Renee Hanover papers, LHA
24   Bernstein, "Homosexual Leader Hits Church"
25   Michael Ferri interview by author, July 24, 1994
26   Paul Breton interview by author, Nov. 17, 1998
27   Breton interview
28   "Gay Power Faces Down 'Doctor' Cavanaugh"

29   GLF flyer from CUA symposium
30   Breton interview
31   "Gay Power Faces Down 'Doctor' Cavanaugh"
32   Lilli Vincenz ms in *Gay* magazine II 2 No. 40, nd
33   "Seminar hostile" (letter to the editor), *The Tower*, Vol. 49 No. 11, Dec. 11, 1970, p. 5
34   "Gay Power Faces Down 'Doctor' Cavanaugh"
35   Vincenz ms in *Gay*
36   "Letter from Franklin Kameny—D.C. uproar," Renee Hanover papers, LHA
37   Vincenz ms in *Gay*
38   "Gay Power Faces Down 'Doctor' Cavanaugh"
39   "Homosexuality Seminar Explores Attitudes"
40   "Letter from Franklin Kameny—D.C. uproar"
41   Bernstein, "Homosexual Leader Hits Church"
42   Breton interview
43   Tom Ashe manuscript, untitled and undated. Courtesy Tom Ashe.
44   "Free the Washington Twelve," press release, nd. Also published in *Gay Sunshine*, Vol. 1, No. 5, January 1971, p. 13.
45   Hearing notes exhibits in Jose Ramos file Nov. 29, 1970
46   Tim Corbett, "Free the DC Twelve," GLF Newsletter, Vol. 1 No. 16, Dec. 1, 1970
47   Tom Ashe manuscript, untitled and undated. Courtesy Tom Ashe. There are different versions of who the two men besides Ashe and Ramos were, as well as variations on their ethnicity. I am trusting Ashe, since he was there at the Zephyr. He lists the others as "Doug, a white brother from Virginia, and Larry, a black brother from Boston." Apparently they were not arrested.
48   Ashe manuscript
49   Ned Scharff, "The New Radicals," *Washington Star*, Jan. 24, 1971, p. D1
50   Ashe manuscript
51   Fred Norris (owner of the Zephyr) interview by author, Nov. 20, 2001
52   "Government Response to a Motion for Expungement" for all 12 defendants, Superior Court of the District of Columbia, signed by Ann S. duRoss, March 1, 1971
53   Ashe manuscript
54   Ashe manuscript
55   Ashe manuscript
56   Tom Ashe, "D.C. Twelve Freed: Gays vs. Government," Liberation News Service, No. 324, March 10, 1971, p. 11.
57   Charles Daniels (member of D.C. 12 defense team) interview by author, July 19, 1999
58   "No More Oppression: Why a Revolutionary People's Constitutional Convention?" free supplement reprinted from *Black Panther* newspaper, nd, p. 7, courtesy Tom Ashe.
59   Bobby Seale, *Seize the Time: The Story of the Black Panther Party and Huey P. Newton* (1970; Baltimore: Black Classic Press, 1991), pp. 61–62
60   This phrase was used in several speeches by Malcolm X, most notably at the June 28, 1964, founding rally of the Organization of Afro-American Unity in New York. Malcolm X, *By Any Means Necessary: Speeches, Interviews, and a Letter*, ed. George Breitman, New York: Pathfinder Press, 1970.
61   Floyd W. Hayes III and Francis A. Kiene III, "'All Power to the People': The Political Thought of Huey P. Newton and the Black Panther Party," in *The Black Panther Party* (Reconsidered), ed. Charles Edwin Jones, Baltimore: Black Classic Press, 1998, pp. 157–176, at pp. 169–170

62   Seale, *Seize the Time*, p. 188.

63   "Message to America, Delivered on the 107th Anniversary of the Emancipation Procla-
      mation at Washington, D.C. Capitol of Babylon, World Racism, and Imperialism, June
      19, 1970, by the Black Panther Party," free supplement reprinted from *Black Panther*
      newspaper, nd, pp. 8-9, courtesy Tom Ashe.

64   Huey P. Newton, "A Letter to the Revolutionary Brothers and Sisters about the Wom-
      en's Liberation and Gay Liberation Movements," New York, Aug. 15, 1970

65   Current Biography, 1973, p. 309

66   Text of speech in Liberation News Service No. 280, Aug. 15, 1970, p. 6

67   Mary Breasted, "U.S. Judge Restrains Police on Violating Panther Rights." *Washington
      Star*, Sept. 5, 1970, p. A1

68   Plenary session handouts, September 1970. Courtesy Tom Ashe.

69   "Revolutionary People's Constitution Convention, Self Determination for High School
      Students Workshop Report, handout, nd. Courtesy Tom Ashe.

70   Lois Hart, "Black Panthers Call a Revolutionary People's Constitutional Convention: A
      White Lesbian Responds," *Come Out!*, Vol. 1 No. 5, September/October 1970, p. 15

71   Martha Shelley, "Subversion in the Womans Movement: What Is to Be Done," *Off Our
      Backs*, Vol. 1 No. 13, Nov. 8, 1970, pp. 5–7

72   GLF Newsletter, Vol. I No. 6, Sept. 15, 1970, p. 2, Box 285073726 (Box 1 of 29),
      Renee Hanover papers, LHA

73   Ferri interview

74   "Gay People Help Plan New World," *Gay Flames*, Issue 2 (New York), Sept. 11, 1970.
      (Folder 16, Bruce Pennington papers, Rainbow History Project Collection, Historical
      Society of Washington). Also reproduced in Donn Teal, *The Gay Militants*, p. 173.

75   "Gays Discover Revolutionary Love," a Chicago Gay Liberation report on the male
      homosexual workshop of the Revolutionary People's Constitutional Convention plenary
      session in Philadelphia, Sept. 20, 1970, ONE National Gay & Lesbian Archives at the
      USC Libraries, courtesy Hugh Ryan and John Knoebel.

76   "Gays Discover Revolutionary Love"

77   Ferri interview

78   Revolutionary Peoples Constitutional Convention and Bay Area Pre-Convention
      information handouts (a Bay Area Regional Conference for Revolutionary Peoples
      Constitutional Convention took place in Berkeley starting Nov. 14), courtesy Tom Ashe.

79   GLF Newsletter, Vol. I No. 13, Nov. 3, 1970, Box 285073726 (Box 1 of 29), Renee
      Hanover papers, LHA

80   Tim Tomasi interview by author, Apr. 11, 1995

81   Ivan C. Brandon and Jim Mann, "Panthers End D.C. Convention," *Washington Post*,
      Nov. 30, 1970

82   Steve Goldberg, "Revolution Seizes AU," *The Eagle* (American University), Dec. 4,
      1970, p. 20

83   Registration form in *Quicksilver Times*, Nov. 24-Dec. 4, 1970, p. 8

84   Brandon and Mann, "Panthers End D.C. Convention"

85   "Statement by the Black Panther Party on the Feeble Attempt of the 'Pigs of the Power
      Structure' to Crush the Revolutionary Peoples Constitutional Convention," press
      release, Nov. 27, 1970, courtesy Tom Ashe.

86   Matt Schudel, "Howard President's Tenure Marked by Turmoil," *Washington Post*, Jan.
      10, 2010

87   "Street Guide," *Quicksilver Times*, Nov. 24-Dec. 4, 1970, insert.

88   Brandon and Mann, "Panthers End D.C. Convention"

89   "GLF Presents Program Despite RPCC Chaos," *Quicksilver Times*, Dec. 8-18, 1970, p. 15

90   Mike Silverstein, "RPCC…" *Gay Sunshine* Vol. 1 No. 5, January 1971, p. 5.

91   GLF Newsletter, Vol. 1 No. 16, Dec. 1, 1970

92   Tom Ashe interview by author, July 31, 1998

93   "GLF Presents Program Despite RPCC Chaos"

94   Notes taken during gay men's workshop in D.C. 1970, courtesy Tom Ashe.

95   Phil Hilts, "Panther Convention Has a Time but No Place," *Washington Daily News*, Nov. 28, 1970, p. 5

96   Steve Goldberg, "Revolution Seizes AU"

97   Silverstein, "RPCC…"

98   Joe Covert, "Christopher Street Spirit Zaps Washington," GLF Newsletter, Vol. 1 No. 16, Dec. 1, 1970

99   "Gays Get Together in Washington," Liberation News Service, No. 301, Dec. 9, 1970, p. 14

100 Robert Taylor, "Panthers Castigate Howard at Convention," *The* (Howard University) *Hilltop*, Vol. 53 No. 10, Dec. 4, 1970, pp.1-6

101 Covert, "Christopher Street Spirit Zaps Washington"

102 Silverstein, "RPCC …"

103 "Revolutionary Peoples' Constitutional Convention: Short Episodes," *Quicksilver Times*, Dec. 8-18, 1970, p. 6

104 "Revolutionary Peoples' Constitutional Convention: Short Episodes."

105 Covert, "Christopher Street Spirit Zaps Washington"

106 "Getting Busted": Gay Busts I: Repression in D.C." by Chicago Gay Liberation from a draft by Step May, *Chicago Seed*, December 1970, no page. Courtesy Tom Ashe.

107 Bruce Pennington interview by author, March 3, 2001

108 John Zwerling (member of D.C. 12 defense team) interview by author, May 5, 1999

109 Tim Corbett interview by author, July 14, 1999

110 Ashe manuscript

111 Pennington interview

112 "Getting Busted": Gay Busts I: Repression in D.C."

113 "Motion to Expunge Arrest Record" of Thomas Michael Ashe, Superior Court of the District of Columbia, submitted by Charles Daniels, Georgetown Legal Intern Program, filed Feb. 23, 1970.

114 Ashe manuscript

115 Scharff, "The New Radicals"

116 Daniels interview

117 "Free the Washington Twelve," press release

118 Ashe manuscript

119 Ashe manuscript

120 Maybauer interview

121 Ashe manuscript

122 Hearing notes exhibits placed in Ramos file Nov. 29, 1970

123 Pennington interview

124 Daniels interview

125 Pennington interview

126 The D.C. 12 were: Richard Chinn, Alfredo Perez, Donald Goldman, Terry Leigh, Michael Goldberger, Jose Ramos, Thomas Ashe, Peter Fugiel, Kenneth Dudley, Timothy Corbett, John Maybauer, Reginald Haynes.

127 Corbett, "Free the DC Twelve"

129 Renee Hanover (member of D.C. 12 defense team) interview by author, Aug. 8, 1999

129 Hanover interview, Aug. 8, 1999

130 Hanover interview, Aug. 8, 1999

131 John Maybauer interview by author, Apr. 28, 1999

132 Hanover interview, Aug. 8, 1999

133 Hanover interview, Aug. 8, 1999

134 Daniels interview

135 "Zapping the Zephyr," no byline but written by Tom Ashe, *Philadelphia Gay Dealer*, ca. December 1970

136 Zwerling interview

137 Maybauer interview

138 Zwerling interview

139 Hanover interview, Aug. 8, 1999

140 Charles Daniels, John Zwerling interviews

141 Daniels interview

142 Maurine Beasley, "4 Homosexuals Freed, Witnesses Doubted," *Washington Post*, Feb. 19, 1971, p. C5

143 Hanover interview, Aug. 8, 1999

144 Zwerling interview

145 Zwerling interview

146 Zwerling interview

147 Zwerling interview

148 Daniels interview

149 GLF press release, Feb. 10, 1971

150 Daniels interview

151 Ashe, "D.C. Twelve Freed: Gays vs. Government"

152 Renee Hanover interview by author, Aug. 15, 1999

153 "Memoranda and Points and Authorities in Support of Defense Request to Inquire Into Homosexual Bias on the Part of Prospective Jurors During Voir Dire," for defendants Ramos, Ashe, Goldberger and Leigh, in Superior Court of the District of Columbia, by Charles Daniels, Feb. 5, 1970

154 Zwerling interview

155 "Memoranda and Points and Authorities in Support of Defense Request to Inquire Into Homosexual Bias on the Part of Prospective Jurors During Voir Dire"

156 Zwerling interview

157 Hanover interview, Aug. 15, 1999

158 Matt Schudel, "Dyer Justice Taylor; Judge Survived WWII Plane Crash," *Washington Post*, Dec. 24, 2008, p. B6

159 Ellen Robertson, "Dyer J. Taylor, Retired Judge, Dies," *Richmond Times-Dispatch*, Nov. 23, 2008

160 Maybauer interview

161 Memo from Hanover to Chicago National Lawyer's Guild, March 1, 1971, Box 285073728 (Box 2 of 29), Renee Hanover papers, LHA

162 Hanover interview, Aug. 15, 1999
163 Ashe interview
164 Ashe interview
165 Ashe interview
166 Hanover interview, Aug. 15, 1999
167 Ashe, "D.C. Twelve Freed: Gays vs. Government"
168 Beasley, "4 Homosexuals Freed, Witnesses Doubted"
169 Daniels interview
170 "Revolutionary Peoples' Constitutional Convention: Plain Facts," *Quicksilver Times*, Dec. 8-18, 1970, p. 6
171 Donna McKeown, "Seeds of Revolution Fail to Sprout at Panther Rally," *Washington Daily News*, Nov. 30, 1970, p. 5
172 "Revolutionary Peoples' Constitutional Convention: Short Episodes"
173 Brian Doherty, "Convention Fizzles," *The Eagle* (American University), Dec. 4, 1970, p. 20
174 Doherty, "Convention Fizzles"
175 John Knoebel interview by author, June 2, 2020
176 Come Out Vol. 1 No. 7, January 1971, p. 16
177 Extrapolated from "Statement of the Male Homosexual Workshop," prepared at the RPCC Plenary Session in Philadelphia, and "Self-Determination for Gay People: Statement of the Homosexual Workshop of the Bay Area Regional Conference of the Revolutionary People's Constitutional Convention." Courtesy Tom Ashe.
178 Silverstein, "RPCC ..."
179 Brandon Jim Mann, "Panthers End D.C. Convention"
180 "Revolutionary Peoples' Constitutional Convention: Huey Speaks," *Quicksilver Times*, Dec. 8-18, 1970, p. 7
181 "Revolutionary Peoples' Constitutional Convention: Huey Speaks"
182 "Huey Newton Asks End to Boundaries," by Austin Scott, *Washington Post*, Nov. 29, 1970, p. D1
183 "Revolutionary Peoples' Constitutional Convention: Plain Facts"
184 Taylor, "Panthers Castigate Howard at Convention"
185 Editorial, *The* (Howard University) *Hilltop*, Vol. 53, No. 10, Dec. 4, 1970, p. 1
186 "Revolutionary Peoples' Constitutional Convention: Short Episodes"
187 McKeown, "Seeds of Revolution Fail to Sprout at Panther Rally"
188 Cynthia Gorney, "Huey Newton, Cofounder of Black Panthers, Is Slain in Oakland," *Washington Post*, Aug. 23, 1989, p. A6
189 "Gay Lib sponsors D.C. 12 lawyer," *Northern Star* (Northern Illinois University, DeKalb), March 17, 1971, p. 2. Box 285073728 (Box 2 of 29), Renee Hanover papers, LHA
190 Janelle Jones, John Schmitt and Valerie Wilson, "50 Years After the Kerner Commission: African Americans Are Better Off in Many Ways but Are Still Disadvantaged by Racial Inequality," Economic Policy Institute (PDF), Feb. 26, 2018, pp. 1-8
191 LaGarrett J. King, "The Status of Black History in U.S. Schools and Society," *Social Education* journal, National Council for the Social Studies, Vol. 81 No. 1, January/February 2017, pp. 14-18
192 Jones, Schmitt and Wilson, "50 Years After the Kerner Commission," p. 2

CHAPTER 6

1   Paul Kuntzler interview by author, July 28, 1998
2   "Mattachine Figure Runs for Delegate," *Washington Post*, Feb. 4, 1971, p. B2.
3   Letter from Frank Kameny to Peter Sorgen of GLF Los Angeles, Feb. 6, 1971, from Kameny papers, Box 92, Library of Congress
4   Bart Barnes, "Kameny Stresses Personal Freedom," *Washington Post*, March 3, 1971, p. B1
5   Undated handout titled "D.C. candidates speak to the gay voter," Box 285073726 (Box 1 of 29), Renee Hanover papers, Lesbian Herstory Archives of the Lesbian Herstory Foundation Inc.
6   Kuntzler interview
7   "Mattachine Figure Runs for Delegate"
8   *Gay Blade*, Vol. 2 No. 5, February 1971
9   Kameny interview
10   Kameny interview
11   Kuntzler interview
12   "A Second Term for Mrs. Norton," *Washington Post*, Oct. 28, 1992, p. A24
13   *Gay Blade*, April 1971
14   Joel Martin interview by author, Apr. 1, 1997
15   The Gay Activists Alliance of Washington, D.C., incorporated in February 1972, per documents of incorporation in RHP website
16   *Gay Blade*, March 1971
17   Thomas Shales, "Gay Liberation in D.C.," D.C. Gazette Vol. 2 No. 16, May 24-June 6, 1971, p. 17
18   Various undated Gay May Day flyers
19   Jim Lawrence interview by author, June 11, 1994
20   Warren Blumenfeld interview by author, Sept. 15, 1998
21   John Scagliotti interview by author, Feb. 15, 1999
22   "May Day is Gay Day: Gay liberation is antiwar movement," Liberation News Service No. 331, Apr. 3, 1971, p. 10
23   Lawrence interview
24   "Mayday: 12,000 Busts Can't Stop the People's Peace," Liberation News Service, No. 340, May 8, 1971, p. 1
25   Paul Valentine, "Officials, Protesters Prepare for Period of Disruption Here," *Washington Post*, Apr. 30, 1971, p. A8
26   Perry Brass, "Gay May Day!" *Come Out*, Vol. 2 No. 7b, Spring-Summer 1971, p. 14. Courtesy Perry Brass.
27   Scagliotti interview
28   "Mayday: 12,000 Busts"
29   Brass, "Gay May Day!"
30   Brass, "Gay May Day!"
31   Paul W. Valentine, "7,000 Arrested in Disruptions," *Washington Post*, May 4, 1971, p. A1
32   Brass, "Gay May Day!" p. 15
33   Lawrence interview
34   "Mayday: 12,000 Busts"

35 Donald Button interview by author, Feb. 4, 2016

36 Deacon Maccubbin interview by author, Sept. 25, 1998

37 "Mayday: 12,000 Busts"

38 Valentine, "7,000 Arrested in Disruptions"

39 Paul W. Valentine, "Mayday Rulings Widened," *Washington Post*, Apr. 17, 1973, p. C1

40 Valentine, "7,000 Arrested in Disruptions"

41 Jack Drescher, "Out of DSM: Depathologizing Homosexuality," *Behavioral Sciences*, Vol. 5, No. 4 (2015), pp. 565–575

42 "Lifestyles of the Non-Patient Homosexual," unpublished, unofficial transcript from the APA panel, May 6, 1971, Phyllis Lyon and Del Martin Papers, Box 40, Folder 40, GLBT Historical Society, San Francisco

43 Kuntzler interview

44 Cliff Witt interview by author, July 21, 1998

45 Kameny interview

46 Kuntzler interview

47 "Peace Gays Confront Shrink Pigs," by a Gay Flame, Liberation News Service, No. 341, May 12, 1971, p. 10

48 Michael Ferri interview by author, July 24, 1994

49 Brass, "Gay May Day!"

50 Witt interview

51 Brass, "Gay May Day!"

52 Kameny interview

53 "Speech for the American Psychiatric Association, handout, May 3, 1971

54 Brass, "Gay May Day!"

55 Warren J. Blumenfeld, "One Year Sick & Then Not: On the Social Construction of Homosexuality as 'Disease,'" The Bilerico Project blog, Feb. 24, 2013

56 Franklin E. Kameny, "A Brief History of the Gay Movement in Washington, D.C.—A Study in Success and How to Achieve It," May 5, 1979, Library of Congress, Kameny papers Box 126

57 Kameny, "A Brief History of the Gay Movement in Washington, D.C."

58 *Gay Blade*, July 1971

59 *Gay Blade* Vol. 3 No. 1, October 1971

CHAPTER 8

1   Michael Ferri interview by author, July 24, 1994

2   Tim Corbett interview by author, Aug. 14, 1994

3   Andy Hughes interview by author, Sept. 15, 1998

4   Ferri interview, July 24, 1994

5   Michael Ferri interview by author, June 4, 2019

6   Kent Jarratt interview by author, Nov. 19, 1994

7   Tim Tomasi interview by author, Apr. 11, 1995

8   Tomasi interview

9   Theodore Kirkland memorial service program notes, May 21, 2009, Washington

10 Turner Brown, *Black Is*, Grove Press, N.Y., 1969

11 Kirkland interview by author, Aug. 12, 1994

12   Jim Lawrence interview by author, June 11, 1994
13   Lawrence interview
14   David Duty interview by author, Dec. 3, 1994
15   Duty interview
16   Lawrence interview
17   Duty interview
18   Kirkland interview
19   Jarratt interview
20   Tomasi interview
21   Lawrence interview
22   Ferri interview, July 24, 1994
23   Tim Tomasi interview by author, Sept. 23, 2016
24   Ferri interview, July 24, 1994
25   Duty interview
26   Tomasi interview, Apr. 11, 1995
27   Tomasi interview, Apr. 11, 1995
28   Ferri interview, July 24, 1994
29   Duty interview
30   Author's journal, Dec. 22, 1971
31   Ferri interview, July 24, 1994
32   Tomasi interview, Apr. 11, 1995
33   Jarratt interview
34   Essay by Ginny Berson, *The Furies Lesbian/Feminist Monthly*, Vol. 1, January 1972, p. 1
35   Berson essay, *The Furies*
36   Tomasi interview, Sept. 23, 2016
37   Sue Fox, "The Furies," *Washington Blade*, Vol. 26 No. 24, June 16, 1995, p. 67
38   Anne M. Valk, *Radical Sisters: Second-Wave Feminism and Black Liberation in Washington, D.C.*, University of Illinois Press, Urbana and Chicago, 2008, p. 144
39   Lawrence interview
40   Ferri interview, July 24, 1994
41   Rita Mae *Brown, Rita Will: Memoir of a Literary Rabble-Rouser*, Bantam Books, New York, 1997, p. 270
42   Will Balk interview by author, July 19, 1998
43   Ferri interview, July 24, 1994
44   Bill Taylor interview by author, July 8, 1997
45   Balk interview
46   Bruce Pennington interview by author, Dec. 29, 1994
47   New York Public Library Archives & Manuscripts website: Roy Eddey (Motive) papers, Biographical/Historical Information
48   Roy Eddey interview by author, May 26, 1996
49   Duty interview
50   Roy Eddey and Michael Ferri, "Approaching Lavender," *Motive*, Vol. 32 No. 2, 1972, p. 3
51   Eddey interview
52   *Quicksilver Times*, Vol. 3 No. 8, Apr. 30-May 13, 1971, p. 2
53   "Community Bookstore," *Quicksilver Times*, Vol. 3 No. 4, Mar 2-15, 1971, p. 5
54   The store had a Gay Liberation section as of August 1971, per *Gay Blade*, Vol. 2 No.

12, September 1971

55 *Gay Blade*, Nov. 1971

56 Balk interview

57 Jarratt interview

58 Newsletter, unmarked but probably Vol. 1 No. 8, Sept. 29, 1970, Frank Kameny papers, Box 92, Library of Congress

59 Ian Lekus, "Queer Harvest: Homosexuality, the U.S. New Left, and the Venceremos Brigades to Cuba," *Radical History Review*, Duke University Press, Issue 89, Spring 2004, p. 77

60 Heidi Steffens, "Revolutions Are Never Easy," *Off Our Backs*, October 1971, p. 36

61 "Venceremos 5 Sign-up Time," *Quicksilver Times*, Vol. 3 No. 19, Oct. 13-27, 1971, p. 9

62 Ferri email, 14 May, 2014

63 "...For a Confrontation With the Venceremos Brigade," by D.C. Faggots, *Quicksilver Times*, Jan. 29-Feb. 10, 1972, p. 9, courtesy Michael Ferri.

64 Nancy Ferro, "The Venceremos Brigade Meets Gay Liberation at the Community Bookshop," *Off Our Backs*, March 1972, p. 5

65 "...For a Confrontation With the Venceremos Brigade"

66 Kenneth Pitchford interview by author, Jan. 31, 1999

67 Pitchford interview

68 Pitchford interview

69 Pitchford interview

70 Steven Dansky, John Knoebel and Kenneth Pitchford, "Principles of Revolutionary Effeminism," *Double-F: A Magazine of Effeminism*, No. 2, Winter/Spring 1973, pp. 3-4

71 Dansky, Knoebel and Pitchford, "Principles of Revolutionary Effeminism"

72 "Don't March! It's Part of a Sexist Plot." By Faggot Effeminists, *Double-F: A Magazine of Effeminism*, No. 2, Winter/Spring 1973, p. 12

73 Dansky, Knoebel and Pitchford, "Principles of Revolutionary Effeminism"

74 Lawrence interview

75 Lawrence interview

76 Ferri interview, Apr. 15, 2014

77 Warren Blumenfeld interview by author, May 24, 2014

78 Warren Blumenfeld interview by author, Sept. 15, 1998

79 Pitchford interview

80 Undated flyer, courtesy Michael Ferri

81 Blumenfeld interview, Sept. 15, 1998

82 "...For a Confrontation With the Venceremos Brigade"

83 Pitchford interview

84 Blumenfeld interview, May 24, 2014

85 Ferro, "The Venceremos Brigade Meets Gay Liberation"

86 Ferro, "The Venceremos Brigade Meets Gay Liberation"

87 Tomasi interview, Sept. 23, 2016

88 Jarratt interview

89 Tomasi interview, Sept. 23, 2016

90 Ferri interview, June 4, 2019

91 Duty interview

92 Lawrence interview

93 Duty interview

94   Michael Ferri interview by author, March 15, 2018
95   Jarratt interview
96   Lawrence interview
97   Jim Lawrence interview by author, Apr. 2, 1999
98   Lawrence interview, Apr. 2, 1999
99   Lawrence interview
100   Lawrence interview
101   Author's journal, March 29, 1972
102   Lawrence interview
103   Lawrence interview
104   Jarratt interview
105   Tomasi interview, Sept. 23, 2016
106   Kenneth Pitchford, "Change or Die," *Double-F: A Magazine of Effeminism*, No. 2, Winter/Spring 1973, p. 25
107   Pitchford, "Change or Die"
108   Pitchford, "Change or Die"
109   Pitchford, "Change or Die"
110   Kenneth Pitchford, "Eighty-Eight—Count 'Em, Eighty-Eight—Reasons Why I Refuse to March Up Sixth Avenue for a Third Time in Pursuit of That Sexist Illusion, Gay Liberation," *Double-F: A Magazine of Effeminism*, No. 2, Winter/Spring 1973, p. 13
111   Pitchford interview
112   Pitchford interview
113   Pitchford interview
114   Ferri interview, July 24, 1994
115   Kirkland interview
116   Tomasi interview, Sept. 23, 2016
117   Tomasi interview, Apr. 11, 1995

CHAPTER 9

1   "Gay Lib Group Seeks Official Recognition." *The Hatchet* (GWU), Vol. 68 No. 10, Oct. 14 1971, p 7.
2   Personal Data sheet, Folder 38, Bruce Pennington papers, Rainbow History Project Collection, Historical Society of Washington, D.C
3   "Gay Lib Group Seeks Official Recognition"
4   Vicky Daunas, "Bringing Gays & Straights Together," *The Hatchet* (GWU), Vol. 68, No. 15, Nov. 1, 1971, p. 3
5   *Hatchet* Vol. 68, No. 23, Dec. 6, 1971, p. 1
6   Steve Behrens interview by author, Feb. 25, 1996
7   Richard Lewis email to author, Jan. 24, 2010
8   *Gay Blade*, Vol. 4 No. 2, Nov. 1972
9   Warren Blumenfeld interview by author, May 24, 2014
10   Warren Blumenfeld interview by author, Sept. 15, 1998
11   Warren Blumenfeld guest blog, "The Gay Liberation Front & Moving Beyond Assimilation," The Bilerico Project/LGBTQ Nation website, May 30, 2014
12   Blumenfeld blog, "The Gay Liberation Front & Moving Beyond Assimilation"

13   Blumenfeld interview

14   Warren Blumenfeld interview by author, May 24, 2014

15   Jay Mathews, "Homosexual Haunt Probed," *Washington Post*, Jan. 3, 1972, p. B1

16   Jerry Oppenheimer, "Gay Activists Battle for Iwo Jima," *Washington Daily News*, Jan. 6, 1972, p. 5

17   Mathews, "Homosexual Haunt Probed"

18   Jay Mathews, "6 Arrested in Protest at Monument," *Washington Post*, Jan. 6, 1972, p. D2

19   David Braaten, "6 Arrested in Gay Protest," *Washington Star*, Jan. 6, 1972

20   Bill Taylor interview by author, July 8, 1997

21   Ken Ringle, "Iwo Jima Monument Grounds Have a Darker Attraction," *Washington Post*, Oct. 7, 1976, pp. C1

22   Gay Pride Bulletin No. 1, handout, nd

23   Gay Pride Bulletin No. 1, handout, nd

24   D.C. Gay Pride Committee's program notes for the Rhinestone Review, May 2, 1972, from RHP collection

25   *Quicksilver Times*, May 5-25, 1972, clipping from RHP collection

26   Program for the Rhinestone Review, May 2, 1972, from RHP collection

27   Paul Hodge, "Open Display of Affection Asked by Gay Liberation," *Washington Post*, May 6, 1972, p. B2

28   Hodge, "Open Display of Affection Asked by Gay Liberation"

29   *Gay Blade*, mid-May 1972

30   Gay Pride Bulletin No. 1, handout, nd

31   Author's journal May 7, 1972

32   Comments by Bruce Pennington, Rainbow History Project presentation, undated author notes

33   "Gay Pride Week Rally Set in Lafayette Park," *Evening Star*, 5 May 1972, no page number

34   Deacon Maccubbin interview by author, Sept. 25, 1998

35   Ruth M. Bond, "The Deacon of Dupont Circle," *Washington City Paper*, Oct. 25, 1991, p. 26

36   Maccubbin interview

37   "Switchboard," *Washington Free Press*, July 2, 1970, p. 2

38   *Gay Blade*, December 1974, p. 5

39   *Gay Blade*, Vol. 4 No. 6, March 1973, p. 5

40   Richard Woods interview by author, Dec. 8, 1998

41   The clinic began operation in 1968. (B. J. Phillips, "Washington Free Clinic: Where Youth and Doctors Meet," *Washington Post*, Dec. 17, 1969, p. C1) It closed in January 2007. (Susan Levine, "After 39 Years, End of a Health Institution: Washington Free Clinic Bids City Farewell," *Washington Post*, January 14, 2007, p. C3)

42   Author's journal, Aug. 3, 1972

43   Bruce Pennington interview by author, Dec. 29, 1994

44   *Washington Blade*, Oct. 13, 1989, p. 29

45   Betty James, "School Editors Press Campaign to Combat VD," *Washington Evening Star*, Sept. 13, 1972, p. 33

46   "Gay Men's VD Collective," *Gay Blade* Vol. 5 No. 12, September 1974, p. 5

47   Per the Whitman-Walker website: In 1977. Clinic leaders separated from the Washington Free Clinic and began to develop their vision for a new, diverse health care organization; Whitman-Walker Clinic was officially chartered on Jan. 13, 1978. In October, Whitman-Walker Clinic opened a new, rented facility at 1606 17th St. NW.

48   Paul Breton interview by author, Nov. 17, 1998

49   Breton letter to Rev. Troy Perry, 30 July 1971

50   Medsger, Betty, "Homosexuals Seek Church," *Washington Post*, Sept. 14, 1970, C1

51   Breton interview

52   Per Metropolitan Community Church website

53   Paul Breton email, Feb. 3, 2003

54   David R. Boldt, "Bishop's Order Disrupts Homosexual Church Plan" *Washington Post*, Feb. 13, 1971

55   "Homosexual-Oriented Worship Service Is Held," *Washington Post*, Feb. 15, 1971, p. A26

56   Rev. Jack Isbell interview by author, May 3, 2003

57   Paul Breton interview by author, March 1, 2003

58   Breton email, Feb. 3, 2003

59   Bulletin from MCC-DC service of 2 May 1971

60   *Gay Blade*, Vol. 4 No. 6, March 1973, p. 1

61   Per the MCC-DC website

62   Dignity DC website; *Gay Blade*, September 1972

63   Per GMCC website

64   Just Us: A Directory of the Washington Gay Community, published by the Washington Area Gay Community Council, 1975, p. 8. Bruce Pennington papers, RHP

65   Michael Ferri interview by author, July 24, 1994

66   Phil Herbert interview by author, March 3, 1996

67   "Swishboard," *Gay Blade*, Vol. 4 No. 12, Sept. 1973, p.16

68   Robert Mott, "Life Becomes Somewhat Easier for D.C. Homosexuals," *Washington Post*, Apr. 23, 1973, p. C1

69   Mott, "Life Becomes Somewhat Easier"

70   *Washington Post* ads, March 1972-April 1973

71   Ferri interview

72   Blumenfeld interview

73   Kennedy Center opened September 1971 per its website

74   Boris Weintraub, "Gay Plumage for Bette," *Washington Star*, March 12, 1973, p. C1

75   Tom Shales, "How Divine: Miss M," *Washington Post*, March 12, 1973, p. B1

76   Weintraub, "Gay Plumage for Bette"

77   Shales, "How Divine: Miss M"

78   Shales, "How Divine: Miss M"

79   Shales, "How Divine: Miss M"

80   Mott, "Life Becomes Somewhat Easier"

81   Jim Lawrence interview by author, Apr. 2, 1999

82   Blumenfeld interview

83   "2018 LGBTQ Youth Report," Human Rights Campaign, hrc.org

84   Amy Ellis Nutt, "Survey finds widespread feelings of fear and rejection among LGBTQ teens," *Washington Post*, May 15, 2018, p. A6

85 "2018 LGBTQ Youth Report," Human Rights Campaign, hrc.org

86 Tony Jackubosky, "Gay Activist Group Formed," *D.C. Gazette*, Vol. 2 No. 18, June 21-July 4, 1971, p. 14

87 Don Wright interview by author, Sept. 23, 1998

88 Thomas Shales, "Gay Liberation in D.C." *D.C. Gazette* Vol. 2 No. 16, May 24-June 6, 1971, p. 17

Acknowledgments

During this 25-year project, my primary thanks must go to my primary sources, those individuals, activists and witnesses, who agreed to interviews (some repeatedly), with special thanks to those who saved historical materials and shared them with me. My interviewees include:

Bill Anderson, Aug. 5, 1998

Tom Ashe, July 31, 1998

Dirk Bakker, Apr. 29, 2003

Will Balk, July 19, 1998

Paul Bartels, Aug. 9, 1998

Steve Behrens, Feb. 25, 1996

Deane Bergsrud, May 9, 1996

Warren Blumenfeld, Sep. 15, 1998; May 24, 2014

Paul Breton, Nov. 17, 1998

John Broere, Sep. 12, 1998

Charlotte Bunch, Oct. 31, 2016

Don Button, Feb. 18, 1996; Feb. 4, 2016

Wade Carey, Aug. 15, 1996

Tim Corbett, Aug. 14, 1994; July 14, 1999

Charles Daniels, July 19, 1999

Nick DeMartino, Apr. 15, 1996

Betsy Donahoe, Nov. 22, 1998

Jonas Dos Santos, Aug. 18, 2014

David Duty, Dec. 3, 1994; Sep. 27, 2019

Roy Eddey, May 26, 1996

Michael Ferri, July 24, 1994; March 15, 2018; June 4, 2019

Jim Fouratt, Nov. 21, 1998

Eva Freund, Jan. 28, 1999

Renee Hanover, Aug. 15, 1999

Link Harper, Aug. 18, 2014

Phil Herbert, March 3, 1996

Andy Hughes, Sep. 15, 1998

Tony Jackubosky, Nov. 11, 1998

Kent Jarratt, Nov. 19, 1994; Sep. 13, 2016
Frank Kameny, May 11, 1996
Theodore Kirkland, Aug. 12, 1994
John Knoebel, June 2, 2020
Paul Kuntzler, July 28, 1998
Michael Lally, March 6, 1999
Jim Lawrence, June 11, 1994; Apr. 2, 1999
Richard Lewis, Jan. 24, 2010
Deacon Maccubbin, Sep. 25, 1998; Dec. 3, 2019
Joel Martin, Apr. 1, 1997
John Maybauer, Apr. 28, 1999
Max Maynard, March 21, 1999
Ron Morgan, May 20, 1996
Bruce Pennington, Dec. 29, 1994; March 3, 2001
Kenneth Pitchford, Jan. 31, 1999
Patrick Rosenkjar, May 11, 2018
John Scagliotti, Feb. 15, 1999
Richard Schaefers, Apr. 29, 1996
Robbie Skeist, Aug. 9, 1998
Otis "Buddy" Sutson, Sept. 8, 2018
Bill Taylor, July 8, 1997
Tim Tomasi, Apr. 11, 1995; Sep. 23, 2016
Nancy Tucker, July 22, 2014
Lilli Vincenz, Aug. 15, 1998
Brenda Wilson, Dec. 10, 1998
Cliff Witt, July 21, 1998
Richard Woods, Dec. 8, 1998
Don Wright, Sep. 23, 1998
Michael Yarr, Aug. 25, 1996
John Zwerling, May 5, 1999

and others who wished to remain anonymous, or with whom I
had shorter conversations.

Thanks to the Rainbow History Project of Washington, D.C., which provided access to archived materials stored at the Historical Society of Washington, D.C.; oral histories (including those of James "Juicy" Coleman, Peter Jefts, Patricia Hawkins, Stephen Miller and Nancy Tucker); a Places & Spaces database; publications on various topics; and other resources. Thanks to the Rev. Candace Shultis of the Metropolitan Community Church of Washington, who let me explore the church's historical archives. Other significant sources of archived materials were the Franklin Kameny Papers at the Library of Congress, and the Renee Hanover Papers at Herstory Lesbian Archives, Brooklyn. I was also able to obtain records about defendants in the D.C. 12 case at the Superior Court of the District of Columbia.

Thanks, finally, to editor, photographer and researcher Steve Behrens, without whose help this history would not have gotten off the ground; editor Michael Gnat; cover designer Eric Seidman; and book designer Judy Walker; with special thanks to Perry Brass, Philip Clark, Nancy McKeon and Robert Wilson, all of whom provided valuable editorial guidance and advice.

Index